FIAF SUMMER SCHOOL
Berkhamsted, 5 July 96

To Karin,

With my very best wishes
for your future in audio-
visual archiving — and
with many thanks for
making th FSS a success.

Henning

KEEPERS OF THE FRAME

THE FRAME

The Film Archives

PENELOPE HOUSTON

BFI PUBLISHING

First published in 1994 by the
British Film Institute
21 Stephen Street
London W1P 1PL

The British Film Institute exists to encourage the development of film, television
and video in the United Kingdom, and to promote knowledge, understanding and
enjoyment of the culture of the moving image. Its activities include the National Film
and Television Archive; the National Film Theatre; the Museum of the Moving
Image; the London Film Festival; the production and distribution of film and video;
funding and support for regional activities; Library and Information Services; Stills,
Posters and Designs; Research; Publishing and Education; and the monthly *Sight and
Sound* magazine

British Library Cataloguing-in-Publication Data.
A catalogue record for this book is available from the British Library.

ISBN 0–85170–470–0
      0–85170–471–9

Cover by Design & Art
Cover frame stills from *La Biche au Bois* (Jacques Ducom, Fr. 1896,
60 mm Demeny).
Typeset in Bembo by Garden House Press Ltd, Perivale, Middx.
Printed in Great Britain by The Trinity Press, Worcester

For the staff of the
National Film and Television Archive,
present and past

CONTENTS

ACKNOWLEDGMENTS

I am grateful to a number of people who have helped me with this book. To Ed Buscombe, who first suggested and then commissioned a book about the film archives, and to Wilf Stevenson and the British Film Institute for enabling me to carry out the research. To many people on the staff of the National Film and Television Archive who have advised me and allowed me to take up their time, but especially to Clyde Jeavons, the Curator, Anne Fleming, the Deputy Curator, Kathleen Dickson, the Curator's assistant, and Dr Henning Schou, head of the NFTVA's John Paul Getty Jnr. Conservation Centre at Berkhamsted. To Robert Daudelin, the President of FIAF, for allowing me to attend the 1992 FIAF Congress, and to Manuel Martínez Carril and the Cinemateca Uruguaya for their most generous hospitality in Montevideo. To Livio Jacob and the organisers of the Giornate del Cinema Muto for inviting me to Pordenone. To Christian Dimitriu and the Cinémathèque Suisse for the opportunity to attend their Lausanne seminar on film preservation, and for their hospitality. To Brigitte van der Elst, executive secretary of FIAF, for her kindness in enabling me to work on FIAF/Lindgren files in her office; and to Mary Lea Bandy and the very helpful staff of the MOMA Film Department in New York for letting me investigate their collection of Iris Barry papers.

Although there are many articles on subjects of concern to the archivists, and a number of technical manuals on questions of film preservation, I know of only two more general books on the subject: Anthony Slide's *Nitrate Won't Wait* (McFarland and Co, 1992), about the history of film preservation in the United States, with a great deal of detail on the history and operations of the American organisations, and information on many of the smaller and more specialised libraries and collections; and *Les Cinémathèques* (Editions L'Age d'Homme, 1984), Raymond Borde's account of the film archive movement, which includes a useful summary of the various initiatives that preceded the setting up of the first archives, as well as much detail on the French archives and the workings of FIAF. I am grateful to M. Borde for sending me copies of some recent, so far unpublished papers, from which I have quoted in the text.

I would also like to thank the various people I have interviewed or talked to, who were unfailingly informative: Michelle Aubert, Peter von Bagh, James Ballantyne, Mary Lea Bandy, Stephen Bottomore, Eileen Bowser, Harold Brown, Kevin Brownlow, Steve Bryant, Elaine Burrows, Ian Christie, Gabrielle Claes, David Cleveland, Tony Cook, João Benard da Costa, José Manuel Costa,

Brigitte van der Elst, Anne Fleming, David Francis, Kay Gladstone, Anne Hanford, Michael Henry, Jane Hockings, Jan-Christopher Horak, Clyde Jeavons, Brian Jenkinson, Christine Kirby, Wolfgang Klaue, Jerome Kuehl, John Lucas, Alain Marchand, David Meeker, Ismail Merchant, Ib Monty, Geoffrey Nowell-Smith, Eva Orbanz, Enno Patalas, James Patterson, David Puttnam, David Robinson, Deac Rossell, Markku Salmi, Henning Schou, Ronald Simon, Anthony Smith, Roger Smither, Wilf Stevenson, Olwen Terris, J. D. Turner, Paolo Cherchi Usai, Professor Donald Cameron Watt, Victoria Wegg-Prosser, Murray Weston.

Thanks also to Kevin Patton (NFTVA Conservation Centre) and Michael Caldwell (BFI Stills, Posters and Designs) for providing the frame stills for the cover.

Film transport at the NFTVA's nitrate storage centre at Gaydon, in Warwickshire

INTRODUCTION
Fragile, Expensive and Dangerous

Years ago, I was sitting in a preview theatre idly waiting for a press show to get under way. My neighbour was one of our more distinguished critics, someone who had been writing about films with great perception and elegance for upwards of twenty years. As the lights dimmed, he leant over. He had been considering the question of how the picture actually arrived on the screen. Did I know about such things? He had noticed that there always seemed to be a beam of light coming from the back of the cinema. Might this perhaps have something to do with it?

This, admittedly, was an extreme case. This was a writer who could cope with the finer points of a film more readily than with some of the practical details of getting from place to place. But it is useful to be reminded occasionally of what film basically is. It's everything we always say it is: the entertainment medium which sometimes entertains, and the commercial property; on rare occasions the work of art; a significant part of the historical record; the way most of us have picked up rather more than we might like to acknowledge about the world and its twentieth-century doings, so that we travel as tourists checking up on what we expected to find rather than as adventurers, and have relied on the cameras for our images of war, from the bullock carts of the Boer War to the oil fires of the Gulf. The sounds and voices of films are as inescapably familiar as the images. *Round up the usual suspects... Nobody's perfect... I think it would be fun to run a newspaper...* One might uncomfortably suspect that more people would be able to identify such scraps of dialogue than could quote you the opening line of Wordsworth on Westminster Bridge or the first sentence of *Pride and Prejudice*. Films make up a major and enduring part of the collective memory of the century.

But film is also something that reaches the screen by way of a beam of light from a projector, and that has to be transported in bulky metal or plastic cans. The first century of cinema has seen the most spectacular advances in communications technology, in miniaturisation and the techniques for the storage and retrieval of information. But at the end of it, rather surprisingly, film itself remains much where it was at the beginning: the thin ribbon of images, housed on an unstable substance with less staying power than paper or parchment, spooled up and packed away in cans.

One day, it may all be on laser disc, and the purists among the world's film archivists may well protest in vain. But not yet. Back in the 1980s, one of the promises of high-definition television was that films would be beamed directly to

1

cinemas, if such places still existed; bypassing all the labour of making multiple prints and transporting them around the country. But this technology also remains just around the corner, not yet capable of delivering in ordinary working circumstances and on a cinema-size screen the quality expected from the best 35mm prints and projection.

Film is fragile, expensive to store, and can be dangerous. It began badly, with a fire in 1897 at the Paris Charity Bazaar which killed 180 people. Nitrate can ignite even in the care of archivists; there have been serious fires at, among other places, the Cinémathèque Française in Paris, Eastman House at Rochester, New York, and particularly disastrously, the Cineteca Nacional in Mexico City, when lives were lost and much of the Mexican film record burnt. In 1993 a nitrate fire at a laboratory in South London destroyed films from the National Film and Television Archive, among others. It takes a cynical archivist to argue, as some actually do, that fires and disasters make good publicity for their profession. But they are a reminder that nitrate, on which all feature films up to about 1950 were shot, is hazardous stuff, that preserving a film heritage is no easy business.

Everyone agrees that it should be kept, and when a popular film (or more often these days a television programme) turns out to have gone missing, there is usually a bit of an outcry. If you have regarded Dixon of Dock Green or Alf Garnett as part of your own past, you won't want to think that the BBC has been careless enough to mislay such relics. Most people probably have a vague sense that anything of significance made for either cinema or television is being kept in safe hands, without giving much thought – why should they? – to the problems and expense of keeping it, or the policies followed by those who take it in, inspect it, ticket it, stack it on shelves, and allow us to take it out and look at it now and again, if we can produce the proper credentials.

The film archivists belong to a young profession. There was nothing that could properly be called an archive until the mid-1930s, and in the early days there might have been some hesitancy about what they should call themselves. Ernest Lindgren was curator of the National Film *Library* when in 1948 he wrote an article for the *Penguin Film Review*. 'The word "archive" rings with a deathly sound in the world of cinema, which is so young and vital and dynamic, eager for the future and impatient of the past,' he wrote with a certain wistfulness. But eight years later, when middle-aged and tired might have seemed more appropriate adjectives for cinema itself than young and vital, the Library had become the National Film Archive (and remained so until 1993, when it recognised its expanded concerns by changing its name to the National Film and Television Archive).* The word library suggests books; the film libraries so-called mostly exist for commercial purposes – stockshot, newsreel and so on. To maintain an often precarious and difficult relationship with the film industry, the archives had to demonstrate their distance from the profit motive, from any suggestion that

---

*At the risk of some confusion, but unavoidably, the Archive is referred to by all three of its names, according to the period under discussion.

2

they might intend to lend out films for money. They chose a name which suggested solidity and safe-keeping.

The preservationists in the archives occupy the moral high ground: their work is fundamental, the bedrock on which everything else rests, and they know it. Unfortunately, they can hardly hope to make it seem dramatic or exciting, although to visit vaults cut into a mountainside or built like cathedrals for cinema, with the stuff of legend piled high above one's head, is at least exhilarating. But as the film archives have grown in confidence, which was essentially a development of the 1980s, have acquired greater official recognition and improved their relationships with the world's film industries, they have also run up against the decline in public service values, privatisation, the recession and the efforts everywhere to reduce public spending. Preservation is the costly and least visible part of the exercise, with nothing much on the surface to show for itself. The demand has been that the archives should be seen to justify their existence by bringing out their films. They feel that they must be seen to be doing something, whatever that something might be. In the late twentieth century there is probably no archive, however small or poorly funded or ill-equipped for showing anything to anyone, which would dare to proclaim that its one concern is with the well-being and proper storage of its collection.

This relatively recent change of emphasis follows a long period in which the archivists were extremely poor publicists for their own cause. (In many ways they still are, being unused to thinking in such terms.) Their problem has always been that they were not the proprietors of most of the material in their care. Film companies presented them with prints of films, but on strict conditions and with limitations on what could be done with them in the way of copying and screening. The rights remained with the donors of the films, or whoever inherited or acquired them, and any suggestion that archives were exploiting their holdings for their own benefit could have been followed by swift reprisals. Companies can, and do, remove their films from the archives, for all sorts of reasons, because they are still *their* films. Also, every archive probably has some material of uncertain provenance, films picked up from private collectors or from outside the system of heavily policed industry control. The safest policy was to keep quiet and attract no unwelcome attention. Undoubtedly, the development of the film archive movement was held back by fear, by an apprehension, often but by no means always justified, that any rash move might jeopardise the all-important relationship with the film trade. In the last decade they have emerged, as it were, from hiding.

The archives have also tended to say nothing much about situations which they knew they could not change. It took Martin Scorsese to alert both the general public and his fellow film-makers to the hazards of colour fading. The archivists could have trumpeted the case as loudly – though probably nothing like as effectively – if they had cared to. Their own attention, however, was focused on the job of copying their nitrate holdings, transferring to acetate stock films which they thought were unlikely to survive beyond the end of this

3

century. It is immensely more expensive to ensure the preservation of colour films, and to have started a hare in this direction might merely have aroused expectations which they could not hope to satisfy.

It has been much the same, more recently, with the vinegar syndrome, the name given to a new and unexpected hazard which only began to show itself as far as the Western archives were concerned in the late 1980s. When cans of film from the 1950s and 60s (post-nitrate, in other words) were opened, a few gave off a strong whiff of vinegar. This was the first sign that decay was setting in, although it had always been assumed that acetate was altogether more durable than the nitrate it had replaced. In working on this book, I have found that many people outside the film world are well aware of the problems posed by nitrate: that it's unstable, highly inflammable, burns ferociously if it takes fire, has to be stored in special conditions, and so on. But no one in the outside world, and not too many of the film-makers and critics I spoke to, had even heard the expression vinegar syndrome.

It is no wonder, in this case, that the archivists have kept quiet. Since the 1940s, those archives which have had the means have been copying their nitrate holdings on to acetate, as the originals came to the end of their life. They had, and still have, no choice. If a nitrate film is to be preserved beyond the death of the original print or negative, it must be copied on to a substance which, it is now known, may prove to be equally short-lived. The symptoms do not as yet affect many films, and there are reassurances that prints made by the archives themselves and always properly stored have a much better survival rate than those which have been given a rough time in cinemas. But undoubtedly the discovery of the vinegar syndrome shifted the ground under the archivists' feet. It showed, if nothing else, how difficult it must always be to predict anything with certainty in an area where the materials themselves are less than a century old.

There have been many changes in the situation of the film archives since the mid-1980s, and in what is very much an international movement they seem to apply to the larger and more settled archives throughout the world. There is much talk everywhere about the 'film heritage', the 'cultural patrimony' and the need to ensure its preservation. At the same time, partly because the archives have kept themselves to themselves, there is little general awareness about the history of the archive movement, about its many current problems, or about preservation policies which have been almost exclusively concentrated on the first fifty years of cinema, the nitrate era. The thinking behind this book is that these are matters of public concern, that since there is a 'heritage' at stake, it would be an advantage to know a little more about what is happening to it.

From the early 1930s, when the archive movement was just stirring into life, there were people who realised that they were embarking on an undertaking which could not be sustained effectively without public funding. The National Film Library, as it then was, had to keep going in its early years on a budget which now looks nothing short of pathetic; but it was public money, giving some assurance of continuity. The Library, like the British Film Institute of which it has always been a part, was essentially a creation of the 1930s and of the public service

4

ideals of that age. It could be seen as some sort of tiny relation of the BBC; it was a contemporary of the GPO Film Unit.

In the economic and cultural climate of the 1990s, a dilemma for the archives is that they can hardly be regarded as likely candidates for privatisation. However hard they work to make their activities seem more openly attractive to the public, by offering greater access, by pursuing the popular role of producing handsomely restored versions of classic films, they are still stuck with the cost of film (and television) preservation. This is an expensive business; and bound to become even more so.

All around the world, however, public resources have been harder to come by. The East European archives, once safely entrenched within state cinema complexes and so well provided for, were thrown out into the cold with the collapse of the systems which supported them. In America, near-bankrupt city administrations have no longer been able to offer funding. The archives may find themselves increasingly thrown back on the need to attract sponsorship (which is also a declining resource, since the lavish days of the 1980s). The temptation will be to concentrate on the showcase activities, such as film restoration, which show them in their brightest light. They cannot, as an art gallery might do, simply clamp down for a year or two on new acquisitions. The flow of material keeps coming, as more and more companies and organisations appreciate the virtue of having their films stored securely – and, it has to be said, at public expense. And the nitrate film still has to be copied to meet its expiry deadline.

If I have somewhat concentrated in this book on the National Film and Television Archive, this is not because I regard it as typical. Several people warned me, with reason, that there was no such thing as a 'typical' archive. The hundred or so organisations which are members of the International Federation of Film Archives (FIAF) may face many of the same problems, but they are not necessarily finding the same solutions, or even looking for them. They vary too much in their origins, scale, structures, funding and the state of development they have reached. Many archives exist independently, but many do not. An archive may be part of a film institute, as in Britain and Sweden (though the two institutes are also very different in their aims and policies); it may be attached to a university (UCLA) or a museum (the departments of film at the Imperial War Museum in London and the Museum of Modern Art in New York). It is bound to take some of its institutional tone from its surroundings.

The National Film and Television Archive is my home base; I could not have looked into the workings of any other organisation in such detail. But the main reason for concentrating on its history and operations is its standing within the archive movement. Ironically, for a country whose film industry seems to have spent most of its existence staggering defiantly between crises, Britain's film archive is among the most stable, principled and highly regarded. And this has always been the case. It was one of the tiny, elite group founded before the war, when people had only recently come to realise that feature films merited preservation. It has enjoyed rare continuity of management: in almost sixty years, it has had only three curators, Ernest Lindgren, David Francis and Clyde Jeavons, and both Francis and Jeavons had served their time under Lindgren before leaving the Archive and later returning to head it. David Francis went on to run the department of film at the Library of Congress in Washington, a unique double.

Ernest Lindgren has been described as the man who invented the science (or art) of film archiving, and also as the conscience of FIAF. For most of his career, he suffered from living in the shadow of his great rival, Henri Langlois, founder of the Cinémathèque Française. Langlois was the man of legend, the flawed angel of the archive movement (though by some barely considered an archivist at all), who knew everything there was to know about films, loved them immoderately, and by way of his brilliant programming helped to nurture and educate the New Wave generation. They in turn enhanced his glory by proclaiming themselves 'Children of the Cinémathèque'. Ernest Lindgren, by contrast, seemed staid and drab and bureaucratic, someone who would rather keep his films under lock and key. The comparison had to be damning.

At the end of the day, however, there can be no real doubt where the balance of advantage lies. Langlois created a kind of personal marvel, but left behind him a legacy of confusion and mistrust which held up the development of the French archives and kept France largely isolated from the international movement. Lindgren had been patiently constructing an institution, put together to last. The major and significant developments have happened since their deaths (or, as David Francis rather brutally put it to me, 'the good things happened after the characters left'), but they largely depended on the ground rules and the solid base laid down by Lindgren.

I should add that I am not an archivist, and this is a book written from outside a world which is itself something of an enclave within the film community. I have talked to a great many people, inside and outside the archive movement, and been able to sample the workings of FIAF by attending one of its annual congresses. I have learnt a lot and am grateful to all my instructors – though my conclusions of course are my own.

There seems to be a notion in some quarters that there was some golden age of archiving, now in the past. Anthony Slide, in his book on the American archives, *Nitrate Won't Wait*, writes irately about a new generation of 'archival bureaucrats . . . not interested in film preservation, only in self-preservation'. I am not qualified to judge whether this is in fact the American experience, but if such faceless people exist I have been lucky enough to avoid meeting them. My impression is that there is still plenty of dynamism left in the archive movement – and that with the mixture of difficulties and opportunities confronting it, there will need to be.

An archive story. Once upon a time, one of the veterans of the archive movement was chatting to his old friend, Henri Langlois. His nitrate vaults were full to overflowing, what could he do with the films? 'Why don't you dig a hole and bury them?' suggested Langlois. This was duly done: the hole was dug, some films interred, the whole thing covered up again. In the catalogue of the archive, the reference was to 'earth vaults'. Some people thought that the grass grew more lushly, the flowers bloomed more brightly in the area where the films were stored. It was some six or seven years before they thought they had better take a look at what was going on. The 'earth vaults' were excavated. Gas fumed unpleasantly out of the hole; they looked down on some rusty cans and tattered shards of nitrate. The site was quickly covered over again. The flowers continued to bloom as handsomely.

I am assured on the authority of someone who was present at the exhumation that this tall tale is true, that I could name with impunity the archivist concerned, who is still alive. I prefer to think of it, however, as a kind of parable for the sometimes curious world of the film archivists, where so many decisions have to be taken on trust.

I

A NEW SOURCE OF HISTORY

'The cinema is an invention without a future,' announced the Lumière brothers, Auguste and Louis, some time after they had launched the whole thing with their first public screening at the Grand Café in Paris, on 28 December 1895. Georges Méliès was warned off in these terms when he tried to buy the patents from them. And if they thought cinema likely to prove no more than a showman's passing attraction, they would hardly have seen any prospect of permanence for their own tiny films: the cinema's first train arriving at La Ciotat, steaming towards the camera and into history, the baby at his breakfast, the factory workers heading home after the day's shift. The only magic at the time was that people and objects were seen to move; the magic ever since has been in those first, far from fumbling efforts to put the camera in the right place; even more, in the unforced, quite undramatic glimpses into the most ordinary moments of ordinary people's lives. The baby, the breakfast, the bicyclists and bustling women, the station platform on that particular day, remain trapped in time forever, or as long as anyone considers anything on film worth keeping.

The invention without a future rather rapidly began to acquire a past. Almost from the beginning, there were people who realised that there might be something in films of future interest: film-makers, that is, who saw that news value might become historical value, even if only in the cause of promoting their own work. I am indebted to the film historian Stephen Bottomore for two cuttings from the magazine *Photographic News*. The first, dated 18 December 1896, reported that R.W. Paul, the British pioneer, had offered the British Museum several of his 'cinematograph reproductions' – scenes of the Epsom Derby won by the Prince of Wales' horse, of Princess Maud's wedding, of London streets. The Museum was said to be rather perplexed about what to do, not in the habit of rejecting gifts but undecided about where to house this novel present. By the time of *Photographic News*' second story, on 12 February 1897, they had managed to make up their minds: they would take Paul's films and put them in the Department of Prints and Drawings. Stephen Bottomore asked the Museum if they knew anything more about this transaction, but they did not. If they had shown rather more enthusiasm and alacrity in 1896, of course, there might never have been a National Film Archive, merely another department of the British Museum. Paul's film of the 1896 Derby, incidentally, found its way to the Science Museum, where it still is. The print held by the NFTVA, long assumed to be the 1896 race, is now thought more likely to be the Derby of 1898.

La Sortie des Usines Lumière

Then in March 1898, out of a clear sky and with the cinema still months short of its official third birthday, came a paper which must rank as one of the most unexpected and remarkable in film history: a considered, reasoned proposal for the creation of a film archive. The author was a Polish camera operator, Boleslaw Matuszewski; his pamphlet was printed in Paris and titled *'Une nouvelle source de l'histoire'*.

Boleslaw Matuszewski had grasped a point which surprisingly few twentieth-century historians have wanted to take up: the value and potential of film as historical evidence, as a primary source in its own right. He admitted the dis-advantage recognised by all later commentators, that most filmed history was bound to be staged history, 'ceremonies arranged in advance and posed in front of the camera'. The 'beginnings of action, the first movements, the unexpected things happen beyond the range of the camera – just as they escape other means of communication.' But he trusted the resourcefulness of his fellow camera-men, to direct them to the places where history was about to be made and where authority might prefer them not to go. Even in war, cameras could be carried into action, held like guns, and could capture at least a fragment of the battle. He had great faith in film: 'The camera will not perhaps give us the complete history, but at least what it gives us will be incontestable and abso-lutely true. . . It has a quality of authenticity, exactitude and precision which is unique to it. It is the honest and infallible eye witness.'

Here he was perhaps somewhat carried away, in his confidence that film evidence would remain inviolate where still photographs could so easily be tampered with or retouched. A fair number of the early 'actuality' films were in

10

any case faked with various degrees of ingenuity, from the blatant concoction of a Dreyfus Case film put together by Francis Doublier in 1898 to the Boxer Rebellion episode staged by the film-maker in his own comfortably suburban garden. Although such exercises, which could hardly have taken in a ten-year-old, were presumably always intended to be read as illustrations of the news, rather than the news itself.

Matuszewski's archive would not, of course, have had any truck with such material. He suggested that it should be attached to one of the great French institutions, such as the Bibliothèque Nationale or the Museum at Versailles. 'It is necessary to give this source, perhaps a privileged one, the same authority, the same official existence and the same possibilities as the other recognised archives.' He wanted a selection committee to choose the material considered worthy of preservation. The negatives were then to be catalogued and kept locked away in sealed cans. Prints would be made available on conditions to be determined by the committee, though he envisaged that some material might have to be embargoed for a number of years.

His own instinct, however, was all for availability. How pleasant it would be for schoolchildren to watch the passing parade of history, the changing faces of cities, rather than having to make do with a few lines of 'vague description' in books. He had shown one of his own films, shot in Russia, to soldiers at a Paris barracks, and been 'surprised and charmed' at the way they reacted to the unfamiliar sights and ceremonies. He took into account that the equipment for

Attack on a Chinese Mission, the Boxer Rebellion film shot by James Williamson in an English garden.

making and showing films was expensive, but it was steadily coming down in price and might soon be expected to reach a point where even amateurs could afford it, 'and would like nothing better than to contribute to the making of history.' Sooner or later, he was convinced, some major European city would establish such an archive: he was offering Paris the chance to be first.

Matuszewski readily admitted his self-interest. He had filmed the visit of the President of France to St Petersburg in 1897, and incidentally encountered his own proof of film's value as evidence. President Faure was said in some quarters to have been guilty of a breach of etiquette (failing to take off his hat while reviewing a guard of honour, or something of the sort); Matuszewski's film showed that Faure had behaved quite correctly. He had also been a cameraman at Queen Victoria's Jubilee, and had other films he had shot in Russia. This material was on offer to the new archive, and he was prepared to go out and shoot more. And, indeed, did so. Later in 1898, he is said to have shown medical men in Warsaw film of an operation carried out by a leading Paris surgeon, shot in a hospital using only natural light.

If the proposal could be seen in one sense as Matuszewski's effort to advance his own work, in the best tradition of the energetic early entrepreneurs, it was an extraordinarily far-sighted and ingenious one. What makes it so especially captivating is its practicality and detail. No one, of course, showed any serious interest in following up the plan, and Matuszewski himself seems to have disappeared from the record as abruptly as he arrived. At the Pordenone Festival in 1992, I met two Polish researchers who had been inquiring into his life. He was back in Paris, it seems, during 1901, but after that they had been unable to find any further trace of him.

It was a long time before anyone would consider keeping films for anything other than historical record purposes. There were many other suggestions over the years, though nothing as thorough and as lucid as Matuszewski's plan. In a second paper, mainly concerned with the possible use of film for military, scientific and educational purposes, even he recognised that the established organisations would be in no hurry to see the value of a new kind of record: 'I have no illusions that my project will quickly be made effective.'

In 1916, *The Times* reviewed *The Battle of the Somme*, that absorbing mixture of actuality and reconstruction, so pillaged for compilation films that people who have never seen the original have still taken from it much of their sense of the landscape of the trenches. 'In later years,' wrote the reviewer, 'when historians want to know the conditions under which the great offensive was launched, they will only have to send for these films and a complete idea of the situation will be revealed before their eyes – for we take it for granted that a number of copies of them will be carefully preserved in the national archives.'

A year later, the Imperial War Museum was conceived, in that same spirit of commemoration which led to the tomb of the Unknown Soldier and a war memorial on every village green. From the first, it was intended that the Museum would keep the official war films, such as *The Battle of the Somme*, along with all its other records, including the collection of paintings by war artists. The Department of Film at the IWM consequently ranks as the oldest British film archive, though in the early years the problem for both the Museum and the film collection was that it had no proper home. 'The collection has a continuous history, but the archive as such doesn't,' said Roger Smither, Keeper of the Department of Film, to whom I'm grateful for information on the IWM's history. The Museum was lodged for a time at Crystal Palace, then in Kensington. It was many years before it settled in its splendid permanent quarters, the old Bedlam Hospital in Lambeth Road. The film collection itself was actually housed for much of the time at the War Office, under the supervision of a part-time custodian, E. Foxen Cooper, who was also cinematograph adviser to the government.

Foxen Cooper would seem to have had all the instincts of an archivist, even without a solidly based archive to manage. Long before the National Film Library came into existence, he took advice from Kodak about the proper conditions for film storage and treatment, and established practices which, according to Roger Smither, 'do not significantly differ from standards still observed in modern film archives.' He proposed (unsuccessfully) that the IWM should take charge of the preservation of all films of historical interest, and in 1929 he wrote a long article about the historical value of films for *The Times* (attributed only to 'A Correspondent', but known to be by Foxen Cooper).

For Foxen Cooper, as for Matuszewski, the film record represented truth; and truth, as he pointed out, was often arrived at largely by accident:

The Battle of the Somme. Courtesy of Imperial War Museum. (neg. IWM FLM 1672.)

Rescued by Rover.
Two different versions of the same scene, from prints held in the NFTVA.

14

A peculiar feature of the few film records that do exist today and that are considered worthy of preservation is that each one of them appears to have been photographed without any intention of its becoming the record of a historical event. . . . They were placed before the public as items of picture news, and their existence today is a chance incident. . . . So the films which up to now have been considered worthy of perpetual preservation are often those which have been obtained with the least financial outlay, though again and again at great risk of life. There was no synopsis prepared, no producer employed, no artist selected, and no special scenery provided. The occasion was a day in the life of a nation, and the recorder merely a cinema operator.

Foxen Cooper argued a case for the preservation of all kinds of factual film records, as a 'national work at the public expense'. 'Future generations will probably be just as interested in seeing how we lived our everyday lives and enjoyed our sports as they will be to see how we fought our battles and heroically met death.' He thought it would be a good idea to preserve films about birds and animals. And, in one short paragraph of this lengthy article, he noted that there had been as yet 'no general desire' to keep feature films. 'Perhaps one day some international society with sufficient means at its disposal will form a library of the great films belonging to the various periods since cinematography came into being . . . if the negatives are still in existence.'

'If the negatives are still in existence...' An enormous number of them were not, even by 1929. It is generally assumed that some 75 to 80 per cent of all silent cinema has been lost, most of it gone beyond recall unless caches still exist in the unexplored recesses of the archives or in the holdings of private collectors. And most of this destruction happened before the first feature film archives came into existence in the mid–1930s. All archivists have a powerful sentimental attachment to silent cinema, a determination to hold on to any scrap that comes their way, however trivial or rudimentary. They see it as their role to try to make up for the sins of the past, the history of loss and neglect. They are in the business of salvage, without looking to many of its material rewards.

Films disappeared because no one considered it worth the trouble of keeping them after they had served their short time in the cinemas. Efforts were made to hold on to anything with long–term reissue value, but much of the rest slid quietly out of circulation. They were made in all sorts of conditions by all sorts of small companies. The companies went out of business; the laboratories in which the original negatives were stored went broke, or the negatives were worn out by being used as a source of new copies. The National Film and Television Archive, for instance, has three prints of Cecil Hepworth's *Rescued by Rover* (1905), each slightly different. The assumption is that as more prints were needed and the original negative was no longer serviceable, they simply went out and shot the film again.

In the 1980s, archivists were asked to name the films they would most like to recover, and the exercise threw up a sorry tale of losses around the world. Among the titles: *Alam Ata* (1931), the first Indian talkie; *Evangelina* (1913), the first Canadian-made feature, of which only part survives; *The Battle of New Zealand* (1921), the first New Zealand feature; *El Apostol* (1917), made in Argentina and thought to be the first feature-length animated film made anywhere; the Australian *The Story of the Kelly Gang* (1906); the Mexican *Revolución Zapatista* (1914). Not to mention the one missing Garbo (*The Divine Woman*), the one missing Hitchcock (*The Mountain Eagle*), and the lost films by Lubitsch and Murnau and Sternberg and so many others.

This destruction of great tracts of silent cinema was usually a matter of accident rather than design. Producers would not deliberately have killed their own creations, Henri Langlois always insisted; but neither would they have gone out of their way to preserve them. Of later Hollywood attitudes, Langlois joked that producers cherished their collections of often worthless modern paintings while throwing away the real treasures – their films. The whole system of film distribution was also no help to survival. The distributors have always held the central power within the film industry, as the pivot on which the business turns. They have been able to dictate terms to exhibitors and bully producers – and the fact that a single company could function as producer, distributor and exhibitor has not affected this basic balance of power. For the distributors, it was a key principle that all films should always remain within the system and under their control. Outside were assumed to lurk the pirates and predators, ready to snatch the films and profit by them if the distributors relaxed their grip.

It was partly as a consequence of this sense of permanent unease that the destruction of the large number of prints made for a film's initial release became standard industry practice. This also made sound business sense. Scrap merchants and junkmen would take the prints for the small value of the silver that could be extracted from them. (Films were sold off by weight; and in the mid-1930s the metal in the average feature was said to be worth about ten shillings [50 pence].) The alternative was expensive storage of prints unlikely to be needed again, with the risk that copies might wander out of safe-keeping. Consequently, if the original negative and the small number of prints kept for reference and possible reissue went missing, there was unlikely to be much back-up from release prints still in circulation.

The major studios for the most part held on to their material: proud companies such as Gaumont or Disney would not have thrown their own history away. Another source of survival, for the pre-1914 American cinema, was the collection of paper prints (rolls of paper prints of the original negatives) which had been deposited in the Library of Congress for copyright registration and from which it was possible laboriously to re-photograph the original films. (In later years, it was enough for the producers to register copyright by depositing scripts and stills, until from 1942 the Library had the storage space to take in the films themselves.)

Even so, it can seem surprising not that so much silent cinema has vanished, but rather that so much has lasted. The most vulnerable material, the little comedies and travelogues and one-reelers from the early days which there was no real reason for anyone to keep, still found their way into the hands of collectors, people who from the cinema's beginnings snapped up the unconsidered trifles that landed up on street market stalls, were left behind by travelling showmen or abandoned in derelict cinemas.

One such collector, perhaps the most extraordinary of them all, and one who acquired his films by more legitimate means, was a Swiss Jesuit priest, the Abbé Joye, who by 1910 had managed to assemble some 2,000 films. Ostensibly, Joye was using his material for teaching, though he was more probably simply one of the first of the passionate, indefatigable collectors. He died in 1919, after which his films were left to languish away, in time to begin rotting. Eventually, the Jesuits offered them to the Cinémathèque Suisse, which felt that the problems they presented were more than a small archive could handle. In due course, like so much else, the collection reached the National Film Archive. The Abbé Joye was not alone: he merely gathered in more films, more assiduously, than anyone else at the time. For the film industry, however, all collectors were potential pirates, infiltrators of their closed system, even though only the very astute or the very lucky could have got much out of their haul beyond the enjoyment of ownership. The professional pirates were another matter, dealing in the markets in areas such as the Middle East or Africa where Hollywood's writ did not run.

The arrival of sound cinema saw major and now deliberate destruction of silent prints and negatives, junking of a kind not to be repeated until the early 1950s, when nitrate gave way to acetate as the material for film-making and the industry again saw reason to dispose, though much less drastically, of outdated wares. By the 1950s, however, the archives were there to mount rescue operations. In 1930 or thereabouts, the films simply disappeared. Sound conquered the film business more swiftly and more totally than anyone had probably foreseen, and within a very short period it became clear that silent films might as well be written off as a commercial asset. They were not going to make a comeback, or survive as a small enclave within the industry: the decks were cleared for sound.

It is often assumed to have been the sudden death of silent cinema that within a few years brought the first film archives into existence. There had been a number of earlier suggestions that feature films should be collected and preserved, some as tentative as that put forward by Foxen Cooper, many more positive. In his useful book *Les Cinémathèques*, Raymond Borde lists several such projects, and although he concentrated on France he recognised that there must have been others elsewhere. But the departure of silent cinema meant the end of its acting styles, its whole evolved tradition of story-telling and symbolism. It was impossible that there should not be a demand for the preservation of the cinema everyone had grown up with, the first thirty years of what was already recognised as the art form of the twentieth century.

If one looks at the nature of the first film archives, however, it begins to seem that their founding can hardly be explained by quite such an easy generalisation. The first European archive was actually launched in 1933 in Sweden, by Bengt Idestam Almquist, who also wrote about films under the name Robin

Hood. For some reason, perhaps because it was seen as something of a private collection, this forerunner of the Swedish Film Institute was not included among the original Big Four, the founders of the International Federation of Film Archives. These were the Reichsfilmarchiv (Berlin, 1935), the Museum of Modern Art Film Library (New York, 1935), the National Film Library (London, 1935) and the Cinémathèque Française (Paris, 1936). These four archives were founded by very different organisations and people, for very different purposes. They reflect not so much the unity of the archive move-ment – that was to be built up gradually over many years – as its startling diver-sity. None of them had anything specifically to do with the task of preserving silent cinema. They took their character from national attitudes to cinema, methods of funding, views about public service; even more, they reflected the tastes and passions and working methods of the people who created them.

The Reichsfilmarchiv was a state archive, the creation of a regime which had a clearer and sharper understanding than any other in history of the uses and potential of film. Hitler attended its inaugural ceremony, in February 1935. The Nazis used film for demonstrations of authority and national unity (*Triumph of the Will*), for international prestige (*Olympia*), for intimidation (*Baptism of Fire*). Inevitably, their plans for the Thousand Year Reich included a storehouse for national cinema. At a time when the other archives were struggling to launch themselves on tiny budgets, the Reichsfilmarchiv was securely financed, assured of proper storage conditions for its collection. The archive did not, of course, survive the war; its collection was broken up, with the bulk of it finding its way to East Germany.

The Museum of Modern Art also acquired its Film Library (as the present Department of Film was then called) in 1935, although the Museum's founder, Alfred Barr Jr, had for some years been trying to persuade his trustees that film should be added to their responsibilities. Funding for the venture came from a grant from the Rockefeller Foundation. The Library was launched with a state-ment by the President of the Museum:

> The art of the motion picture is the only art peculiar to the twentieth century. As an art it is practically unknown and unstudied. . . . This new and living form of expression, a vital force in our time, is such a young art that it can be studied from its beginnings; the 'primitives' among the movies are only forty years old. Yet the bulk of all films that are important historically or aesthetically, whether foreign or domestic, old or new, are invisible under existing condi-tions. To preserve these films and make them available to the public for study and research is the aim of the new Film Library.

From the outset, the Library's emphasis was therefore on the study of films, not simply their preservation. By 1939 it had acquired its own theatre. Through the work of its distribution library, it was to send out films at low cost to film societies and universities, making it a major force behind the development of film educa-tion in the United States. All of which was in line with the thinking of its first

18

curator, the chirpy and courageous 'Birmingham Sparrow' (as Ivor Montagu described her in his *Sight and Sound* obituary), Iris Barry.

Born in Birmingham in 1895, and educated partly at a convent in Belgium, Iris Barry had done clerical work at the Ministry of Munitions during the First World War. She submitted a poem, successfully, to Ezra Pound's Chicago magazine and gloated over the fee, 'an amazing cheque for £14'. She was 'interested in films to a degree which most of my friends regarded as eccentricity or mania', wrote about them for the *Spectator* and the *Daily Mail*, and in 1925 opened the door of her Bloomsbury flat to find the young Ivor Montagu on the doorstep, calling to consult her about setting up the Film Society. By the early 1930s, she had moved to New York and was taken on by MOMA as a librarian. It was Alfred Barr who, in the words of Alistair Cooke's *New York Times* obituary of her, 'thought she would be better employed doing something about the film collection.' Her own taste was bracingly eclectic – she is on record, for instance, as preferring John Ford's *The Prisoner of Shark Island* to *The Informer*, against all the trends of the time.

In her search for films, Iris Barry did something which would probably never have occurred to the other novice archivists, even if they had had the style or the opportunity to carry it off: she laid siege to Hollywood. With the backing of John

Iris Barry

Hay Whitney, a trustee of the Museum and first president of the Library, she and her husband John Abbott (the Library's manager, but by all accounts no match for his wife in flair and resolution) set off for California. In August 1935, a grand reception was held at Pickfair: Whitney and the Abbotts aimed for the top. They were able to offer the rulers of Hollywood what that insecure industry has always wanted, cultural respectability, the assurance that their work was seen as having permanent value. Once they had persuaded two of the majors, Paramount and Metro Goldwyn Mayer, to agree terms with the Museum, most of the other companies were prepared to fall into line.

Having scored this notable triumph, Iris Barry showed her Napoleonic spirit by embarking almost immediately on the conquest of Europe. Her papers, preserved at the Museum of Modern Art, include her report on her travels. In England, the Abbotts were met off the boat by Charles Laughton and Elsa Lanchester, but complained that it was Derby week and there was no one in London to talk to. They did, however, manage to meet the governors of the British Film Institute: 'Our general impression of them was that they were well-meaning but rather vague, and some members of the board less than wholly disinterested.' In France, she met 'a M. Langlois, who has been given a little money to start a collection of French films.' She reported favourably on the Reichsfilmarchiv ('in our experience [it] has met the problem of preserving films more adequately than any other European country'). She was offered cooperation on everything except her request for a copy of *The Blue Angel*. 'This was refused on the grounds that it was a pornographic film, showing Germany and the Germans in a very unpleasant light and therefore they did not wish it to be shown again abroad.' The Abbotts rounded off their journey in the Soviet Union, including the almost obligatory meeting with Eisenstein.

It was significant that the Library was part of a museum, following its general acquisition policies and with an obligation to put its collection on display. But the cornerstone of the Library's policy was also the relationship it had established with the American film industry. In a 'Report on the Film Library' produced in 1956, Richard Griffith, Iris Barry's successor, noted that it had been almost too successful, 'overwhelmed' even in the mid-40s by so many donations (collections of films with Douglas Fairbanks, William S. Hart and others, as well as its acquisition in 1937 of D. W. Griffith's own negatives and feature prints) that it was continually looking for 'breathing space' to concentrate its attentions on preserving and caring for rather than merely assembling films. The Library no longer had the illusion that preservation was 'not only possible but easy'; ample funds 'were or must be or should be' available for the work. Griffith also suggested that the MOMA Library was welcomed by Hollywood partly because it relieved the major companies of any pressure to do the job themselves, to make their own collections available for what was already becoming a serious educational demand. By 1956 there were 'almost seventy-five accredited film courses in more than fifty universities and colleges'.

Iris Barry had left MOMA in 1951, but remained active in archive affairs through FIAF. She retired to live in the South of France, and opened what would appear to have been a not very successful antique shop. 'A dashing lady,' wrote Alistair Cooke in the *New York Times*, after her death in 1969, 'always long on mockery and short on tact' and one who 'always landed on her own or somebody else's feet'. She had 'done what she wanted and become a public servant'; a comment that would probably have held good for most of the pioneer archivists. She had, there was no doubt about it, style, as well as great influence on her contemporaries. In the 1950s, she came to London to give a lecture, and there is a notably sorrowful and apologetic letter to her in the Lindgren files: 'that slender little audience . . . never have I felt so disappointed and so powerless to do anything about it.'

The international archive network began to establish itself very early. When Iris Barry met 'a M. Langlois' in Paris in the summer of 1936, the Cinémathèque Française was not yet officially in existence; its statutes were signed on 2 September 1936. Later, Langlois' supporters liked to claim (may even have believed) that he had been the first of the archivists, inspiring everyone else, although Langlois himself acknowledged his debt to Iris Barry. In 1936 he was 21 years old; Georges Franju, the co-founder of the Cinémathèque, who was to become such a notable film-maker, was 23. They were two very young men, passionate film enthusiasts, whose first ambition had been to set up their own film club. A friend, the critic and film historian Jean Mitry, gave them a hand and they were able to start Le Cercle du Cinéma. Richard Roud in his biography of Langlois, *A Passion for Films*, says that it was their own idea to move beyond this to the creation of a film archive. Raymond Borde, in *Les Cinémathèques*, suggests that it may have been Mitry who steered them in this direction as well. In any event, Langlois' father had met the proprietor of the trade magazine *La Cinématographie Française*, who agreed to give them 10,000 francs (Roud) or 20,000 (Borde) to establish the collection, and who became first president of the Cinémathèque Française. Langlois' own role was, and remained, that of secretary-general. He, rather than the quieter and more self-effacing Franju, was the publicist and propagandist and spokesman.

Langlois' overriding and unchanging purpose was to show films; and to show, not necessarily to encourage research or discussion. In the early days he made it clear that he wanted no debates at his film club. His first programme, according to Roud, was a characteristic Langlois marathon: Epstein's *The Fall of the House of Usher*, Wiene's *The Cabinet of Dr Caligari*, Paul Leni's *The Last Warning*. There was no time here for discussion, just as with Langlois there would never be time for cataloguing the collection, for developing thorough preservation policies. The film programme was the thing, and the attraction of setting up an archive was a combination of the collector's satisfaction in ownership of his treasures and the impresario's urge to find more material to screen. This was the way the Cinémathèque started and the way it would continue; and Langlois was his own master, as the other archivists, with their links to public institutions, could never be.

The fourth of the original archives, the National Film Library, was founded out of ambitions which were altogether less clear-cut, less personal and passionate. The British Film Institute had been set up in 1933, with a list of

21

objectives which included the creation of a 'repository of films of permanent value', and in 1935 this purpose was duly achieved. The BFI itself, however, owed its existence to a jumble of motives and a particular set of attitudes about the cinema which can perhaps best be described as 'very British'. Certainly the Institute which emerged, after a great deal of debate and shuffling negotiation, was a thoroughly British compromise, funded on a meagre though not inadequate scale with public money but operating as a private members' club. It is the discussion which accompanied the establishment of the BFI, and the attitudes it revealed, that makes its early history an intriguing episode in the record of Britain in the 1930s. If the other three archives could be defined in terms of their relationships with the state, with the film industry, and simply with film enthusiasts, the key relationship for the National Film Library was with the education profession.

2

TRADING WITH THE TRADE

The British Film Institute had its origins in a report, *The Film in National Life*, which was published in June 1932. This very thorough and influential piece of work represented the findings and conclusions of the Commission on Educational and Cultural Films, which had been called together to look into 'the service which the cinematograph may render to education and social progress', and had been deliberating in a leisurely way for more than two years. The Commission, which was unofficial, had picked up a Carnegie Trust grant along the way to finance its operations. Organisations such as the British Institute of Adult Education had made most of the running in setting it up, and its membership was dominated by educationists, though with a small but significant sprinkling of civil servants. *The Film in National Life* was largely written by A.C. Cameron, Secretary of Education for the City of Oxford, and husband of the novelist Elizabeth Bowen. It strongly recommended the creation of some form of national film institute.

As usual in such matters, Britain was lagging behind. A number of countries, including France, Germany and Japan, had already equipped themselves with national organisations concerned with cinema. Even 'godless, Bolshevik Russia' had one, which persuaded the Archbishop of Canterbury that it was not an idea to be encouraged. But from the moment the report was published, it was more or less a foregone conclusion that Britain was about to gain a film institute. The journalist C.A. Lejeune warned the film trade to that effect: they might see the report as no more than 'pompous interference by amateurs', but they were going to have to live with its consequences.

Even the usual stumbling block, the problem of where the money was to come from, was sorted out before the BFI even came into existence. Cinemas were to be charged a special charity tax for screenings held on Sundays. John Buchan, novelist and MP, who was to be one of the early governors of the BFI, was also a director of British Instructional Pictures and so interested in the question of education and film. He came up with the ingenious notion that 5 per cent of the Cinematograph Fund should be used for financing the new institute. The Home Office decided to support the scheme, and modest funding for the BFI was therefore secured. The film trade were by no means pleased that money they saw as theirs was to be turned over to such a cause. The 'uplift tax', they mockingly called it. Before the BFI came into existence, in autumn 1933, with the purpose, among others, of trying to influence and improve public taste in films, the trade went to work.

Throughout the period leading up to the establishment of the BFI, there was quite remarkable press interest in the whole idea, with developments reported in far more detail than one suspects would be the case now. 'The scheme... has probably filled more space in the press than the Loch Ness monster and the return of the Ashes combined,' noted a particularly weary journalist. And if one thrust of the Commission's argument was that cinema was altogether too serious a matter to be left to the film industry, and particularly to Hollywood, most of the press were in full agreement.

John Grierson could be relied on to take his own line. In an article in the *Clarion* (1932), he wrote: 'The politicians, the educationists and the moralists are all very worried about it [the power of film]. It was their prerogative until very recently to have all these influences in their own monopolistic keeping, and now the film has taken their power away.' The inference was that they wanted it back again, echoing a slight but niggling suspicion among the film trade that an institute might be a route towards some form of state influence on production, possibly the steering of films towards national propaganda.

The general press view, however, was dominated by attitudes to Hollywood: that it was either sinful or silly, and quite possibly both. *The Times* complained of a 'degrading and dangerous moral influence', likely to be particularly damaging for 'backward peoples' in the Empire. The popular press was, as always, excitable. 'Britain is called upon to develop, and triumph in, an industry which America has debased,' yelped the *Daily Herald*. The *Economist* was, as usual, urbane. 'It is not occasional impropriety but consistent fatuity which may be charged against the film.' People were avoiding films because of the 'certainty of silliness in 90 per cent of the pictures shown'. The *Morning Post* made a wistful demand for 'something better than Hollywood sentimentality and glamour' for a 'film-conscious generation'. Hardly anyone, it seems, was prepared to stand up for the cinema as it was; the concern, across the board, was for cinema as it might be. There was worry about a rare creature, always referred to as 'the intelligent filmgoer', who was thought to be in need of sustenance and encouragement.

'The abandonment of the film to its own devices and its commercial perversion makes a sad contrast to our sensible handling of radio,' commented the *Observer*. The British Broadcasting Corporation had demonstrated that it was possible to tame one of the wild new media in the public service interest, and in some people's minds the model for the nascent film institute was in fact the BBC. Early suggestions were for a body to be set up in a similar way, with a Royal Charter and a board of governors appointed by the government. But the BBC, which had so rapidly become a national institution, of course owed its position at least in part to its monopoly of radio. There was no risk, or even possibility, that backsliders from the Reithian pursuit of excellence could slip away to the more relaxing pleasures of a commercial radio network.

The film institute was to have no such authority. It was never envisaged that it would make films. It was not going to be offered – and emphatically would not have wanted – any public powers of censorship. When R.S. Lambert, first editor of the *Listener* and one of the chief propagandists for the BFI cause, wrote of a

'National Film Institute occupying a position parallel to that of the BBC in the wireless world', he was being either extremely optimistic or somewhat disingenuous. The institute could lobby for the interests of the 'intelligent filmgoer', provide a storehouse of information, set up committees and groups of supporters in London and elsewhere (which it did, with so many committees and viewing panels, all busily talking to each other, that it attracted a certain amount of press derision). In the early years, a surprising number of its members were clergymen. They, too, had a stake in what was going on, believing that film shows in churches might be one way to haul back vanishing congregations.

The notion that activity of this sort could have any real influence on a national scale, creating a more demanding public for whom 'better' films would then be made, was always a dream. The course of an entertainment industry would not be so easily turned, although the example of the BBC, and the strong 1930s faith in public service values – the ideas of links between social improvement and art made easily and cheaply accessible to the public – may have led optimists at least to hope for the best. Sixty years on, with Hollywood in a position of almost total domination over world markets, and with another backlash against 'degrading moral influences' in full cry, the 1930s ideal has to look particularly forlorn and threadbare.

It was not entirely clear, in any case, just what was meant by 'better' films. John Grierson complained that the 1932 Report had much more to say about administrative matters than about what he felt should be at the centre of everything – getting good films made. During all the debating about the future institute, it seems to have occurred to the protagonists that they ought to find out a little more about what actually went on in cinemas. A posse of observers was sent out to report on the educational content of standard programmes. They returned from this foray into the real world with the news that films were not very educational – although they rather sportingly awarded a few plus points to anything showing unfamiliar locations or exotic customs. What was needed, R.S. Lambert thought, was a new kind of film programme, combining entertainment and instruction 'in the right proportions' and so positively counteracting Hollywood values. This, he assumed, the BFI might be able to bring about. The idea of a 'central authoritarian body', as advocated by a writer in the *Schoolmaster*, trying to inject more educational content into feature films might well have agitated the trade – if they had bothered to take it seriously.

At best, the film industry probably thought that it was in for a fair amount of busy-bodying interference. The trade was determined to take no chances, and during the run-up to the creation of the BFI, its representatives used all their influence and negotiating power to ensure that the new organisation presented no threat. At the end of the day there was to be no Royal Charter (though the *Economist*, admittedly, had suggested that this was always rather an over-large gesture for such a small and modestly funded body). There was to be a different style of board of governors from that first envisaged, with three places out of nine specifically secured for film trade representatives. The BFI was barred from involving itself in industry affairs or in matters of censorship. Its aim, as eventually worded, was 'to encourage the development of the art of the film, to promote its use as a record of contemporary life and manners and to foster public appreciation and study of it from these points of view.' This curiously awkward sentence reeks of compromise, of phrase-making by committee.

The larger public purposes, along with the comparisons to the BBC, had been surrendered somewhere along the way. And if the BFI's founders yielded tamely enough to this scaling-down of their first ambitions, the reason, evidently, was that they knew they had to live with the film trade. Walter Ashley, a journalist who seems to have spent most of his spare time writing letters to the press about the BFI, and who later published an extremely irate pamphlet about it, argued that the educationists had been dabbling in film matters about which they were no better qualified to speak than anyone else. The compromise they arrived at suited both them and the trade. Public interest, as such, had largely gone by the board, and what particularly angered him was the pretence that there was no real difference between the BFI as originally conceived and the enfeebled, scaled-down organisation which was left after all the talking. His arguments probably annoyed everyone so much because there was quite a bit of truth in them. Certainly, injudicious boasting in the trade press that the industry had 'taken control' had to be quickly scotched. This, too, was a bit close to the mark.

The power of the trade was ultimately that they had the films; and the BFI needed them. The Institute's purpose was not only to influence films in a general way (at one point, though happily only briefly, they even thought of a sort of Michelin starring system for approved pictures). More specifically, they were eager to get more teaching films into schools. Elsewhere in Europe, things were much further advanced. France had a flourishing educational network, with some 18,000 schools allegedly equipped with projectors, against a mere few hundred in Britain. Schools were reluctant to invest in projectors because they could not count on a reliable supply of suitable films. All these questions, too, aroused great public interest, though with some comments that the British were uniquely resistant to such developments. However, the 'Middlesex Experiment', which involved taking projectors into some schools in the county, was enthusiastically reported. Children impervious to any other form of instruction were said to remember smatterings at least of information reaching them by way of a film – though this soon came to be recognised as another of the teaching profession's hopeful illusions. 'No More Dunces', declared one particularly exuberant headline.

The Institute, therefore, was both to assemble a collection of films of 'permanent value' and to operate a lending library of instructional material. Of the two, the second task was thought to be the more urgent, and also the one most likely to attract public support. The value of a permanent collection, it was supposed, would only become clear when important films actually began to disappear – as some already had. The film trade, for its part, could perhaps see the chance of a new and lucrative market opening up. Throughout the early days of the BFI, there were these confusions about basic purposes, with the trade resolutely corralling the Institute into an enclave labelled 'culture'. Rachael Low, in *Documentary and*

Educational Films of the 1930s, a volume of her massive *History of the British Film*, summed it up in one scathing sentence. The trade 'managed to confine the Institute to a sort of educational half-world, where it was tolerated with everything from vague goodwill through indifference to contempt as long as it did nothing to interfere with the commercial film.'

The Institute was an organisation which seemed to have been born middle-aged. It only caught up with its missing youth when Denis Forman was appointed as director in 1948. From the governors' papers that survive from the 1930s, one would have little idea that this was any sort of arts organisation, still less one confronting the challenge of an art itself relatively new and only just finding its feet with sound. The talk was much more about procedures, about setting up committees and then worrying that the committees might become too independent and slip out of control. The founders of the Film Society, pioneers in Britain of concern for the 'art of the film', were not very impressed. Ivor Montagu cheekily called his own small organisation the Progressive Film Institute. Iris Barry's comment that some of the governors seemed 'less than wholly disinterested' no doubt referred to the industry representatives.

Nevertheless, there was to be a film library, and Ernest Lindgren, a young man who had joined the BFI as information officer, was put in charge of it. The policies he was to follow were outlined in the first report of the Library Committee – undated, but evidently preceding the launch of the Library. They were much less restrictive than legend often allows. Ideally, the committee recognised, a national library would choose to store everything. 'Any kind of selective system must be unsatisfactory. *Every* film has a historical value of some kind.' It was only because of the practical impossibility of keeping everything that they settled for the next best thing: a selection committee system, with 'no pains spared to obtain the very best advice'. They even added that the selectors should give a reason for choosing a film, something often regarded as a particularly fine Lindgrenian touch. They envisaged, as an admittedly rough guess, that some 400 reels a year (or about 40-50 features) might need to be preserved.

They saw Statutory Deposit as the 'only real solution' to the problem of obtaining films for the Library. Without it, an NFL 'with much to ask and little to give would continually be in the intolerable position of an obligee.' At every stage in the history of the Archive, the extension of Statutory Deposit to include films has been an elusive, ever receding goal, a project prepared, documented, costed, always waiting to be implemented, always seen as just around the corner. Interestingly, neither the original committee nor the many press commentators who also advocated it seem to have foreseen any particular difficulty.

The Committee had consulted experts at the British Kinematograph Society and been advised that projection was damaging to a print, that there should be no screening of a film unless a duplicate copy existed or could be made for preservation. The suggestion was that the preservation copy should be on acetate (safety) stock, and that the nitrate original could then be released as a viewing print.

They were determined to build up the instructional film collection for lending out, with the idea that many films would be freely given to the library by government departments, local authorities, charities and others concerned in non-theatrical film-making. And they wanted to assemble a store of films about the lives of 'primitive, barbaric and orientally civilised peoples within the Empire...before they are overwhelmed by contact with western customs.' In other, less time-encrusted words, they were staking an interest in ethnographic films.

As with the setting up of the BFI itself, the press kept a generally sympathetic eye on developments. Whatever they thought of Hollywood's current output, they recognised that great films had been made, and there was concern at reports that no prints of *Metropolis*, *The Cabinet of Dr Caligari* and *The Covered Wagon* survived in Britain. There were still some doubts about the value of keeping commercial features. The *Birmingham Post* welcomed 'the effort of private initiative to do what, later, the nation may discover to be its duty', but added a curiously double-edged comment. 'Our Edwardian films, when we can see them, are a moral lesson on the crudities of early cinematographic technique. Are not our Georgian films worth preserving as warnings against the dangers of a technique that has far outrun the range of the artists who use it?' The *Scotsman* thought that Mickey Mouse, at least, would prove his stamina with audiences. Only the *Sunday Pictorial* took a magnificently contrary line: 'The art of the film is advancing so rapidly that the preservation of old films can be of interest only to cranks. . . . *Becky Sharp* wipes out any importance any previous films might have, and its own importance will be wiped out in a few years time.'

Alistair Cooke, in an interview (presumably on radio) with the new chairman of the Library Committee, Harry Price, found the most appealing question to ask. 'How many bad films will you keep?' Price assured him that bad films would be kept if they had some point of special historical or technical interest, but this was not quite what Cooke had in mind. 'It seems to me that 1970 would be very grateful for a copy of *Getting Gertie's Garter* – the worst film ever made – simply as a social document.' 'Good gracious, yes,' said Price. Later in the interview, Cooke suggested that 'The biggest danger is that of preserving for posterity bad examples of good style.'

If there is something slightly comical about the early days of the National Film Library, it is because of the part played in its affairs, at various stages, by Harry Price. He was a noted ghost hunter of the day, someone to call in if you suspected that you might have a poltergeist on the premises, or at least one original enough to engage a connoisseur's attention. In this capacity, he founded the Society for Psychical Research. He was also, among many other interests, an enthusiastic, omnivorous film collector. When the NFL was founded, Price gave it a donation of £100 (no mean sum, since in July 1936 the NFL only had £69 18s 2d in its account) and also presented it with his own collection, or the bulk of it. He was rewarded with the job of Library Committee chairman, which he held until 1940.

Harold Brown, who was to become one of the world's great experts on the

Getting Gertie's Garter (1927): 'The worst film ever made,' said Alistair Cooke, but he still thought the young British archive should have a print. It hasn't acquired one yet.

techniques of film preservation, the man who when faced with an insoluble problem in printing up early film would put together his own hand-made machine to solve it, had joined the BFI as an office boy because the future Mrs Brown was already working there as a typist. (What did he think of Harry Price? 'I never met him. I was only the office boy.') On 8 May 1935, Brown set off with Ernest Lindgren for the Society for Psychical Research premises, to pick up the first consignment of films for the Library. Of that first batch, an Italian silent short called *Afra, the African Princess* ranks as acquisition number one in the catalogue. And the Library started as it – and all other archives – would go on. When, many years later, they came to catalogue the film in detail, they found that *Afra* was not the original title, and that although it was only a one-reeler there was a scene missing from the Price print.

Library policy, at this stage, was determined by the Committee. The staff consisted of two people, Lindgren and Brown, neither of whom had any experience of actually working with film. Harold Brown was packed off to the Forum cinema, just south of the Strand and also known as 'the cocoa tin' because of its barrel-like shape, to pick up some elementary tips from the projectionists. In making a join, 'It was a matter of pride to be able to take all the emulsion off with one swoop of the scissors. Then you held the thing up in the air and cemented it together.'

Later, he learnt more from the laboratories used by the Library, which inevitably were the cheapest in London. 'The ladies repairing film now at

29

Berkhamsted still do it in the same way as the negative cutters who taught me at Sydney Wake in Wardour Street.' At the time, more expensive establishments than Sydney Wake were charging one penny a foot for printing nitrate film and twopence a foot for acetate (safety). 'Safety cost twice as much and lasted half as long in projection life.' The reason it was used only for non-theatrical production was that it could not stand up to the wear and tear of cinema projection; it was the development of the altogether sturdier triacetate stock that signalled the end for nitrate. As with many of cinema's technological changes, acetate could probably have been brought into general use much earlier, if it had not been for the industry's habits of greed, parsimoniousness and conservatism.

The Library's busy publicity unearthed some early finds. A print of *The Great Train Robbery* turned up in Glasgow. (Curiously, in all the many press references to this discovery, it was described as starring Mae Murray, an eccentric error which must have originated with the NFL). A small cache of early news film arrived in 1937 from the Paisley Philosophical Society. The Society had borrowed the films for an evening's entertainment in 1900 or thereabouts. They had forgotten to return them; forgotten even to rewind them. The cans had simply been bundled into a cupboard, from which they emerged thirty-odd years later in excellent shape. But the three films which the Library liked to emphasise among its early acquisitions were a decidedly odd job lot: *The Great Train Robbery* (and Mae Murray), the pre-war film of the Delhi Durbar, and an unmistakable Harry Price item, the 'authentic' film of the Indian rope trick.

The Great Train Robbery (1903): A print found in Scotland was one of the National Film Library's first acquisitions.

In April 1936, the Library had sent out its first requests to the film industry for prints of their recent films. The letters, signed by Harry Price, outlined the safe-guards which would protect the donors' rights and ensure that no improper use was made of their films. It was sound policy to flatter the companies about the importance of their work; and the letters trailed an optimistic notion that the Library's existence would help to increase cinema attendances, by attracting those who had previously regarded films as 'something ephemeral and unworthy of serious consideration'. No more than two or three films were requested from any company, which might have been the result of rigorous selection policies or simply a desire not to frighten off the trade by seeming greedy. Among the first batch asked for were *The Thin Man*, *Mutiny on the Bounty*, *Becky Sharp*, *The Informer*, *A Midsummer Night's Dream* and *It Happened One Night*.

The NFTVA has files covering the history of its relations with film donors, going back to these first exchanges of letters. Even a sampling of them is fascinat-ing, because it shows what really happened in the day-to-day dealings between individuals, away from the legends about the beginnings of the archives. The film industry was being asked to absorb two largely unfamiliar ideas: that the material companies had been so ready to discard was thought to be worth keeping, and that to this end they would have to allow their property off their own premises, outside the closed, secure system of distribution. That they reacted so calmly, generally helpfully, is the surest sign that the archive movement had been launched at the right moment.

Certainly, the NFL must have felt tolerably gratified by the trade reactions. Alexander Korda wrote that he 'regarded it as a great honour' that the Library wanted prints of *The Private Life of Henry VIII* and *The Ghost Goes West*: he would make sure they were delivered. General Film Distributors (then the distribution arm of the Rank Organisation) were businesslike and cooperative. The London representatives of the American majors all had to consult their masters in the United States, which they did to varying effect. Warner Brothers answered quickly, with the news that the New York office 'are very much interested in your work'. Warners began supplying prints immediately, and over the years have probably remained the most consistently friendly of the American compa-nies. Fox and Columbia also supplied prints from an early stage. And they could be rather engagingly helpful. When the NFL asked Columbia for a print of *Blonde Bombshell*, they were obligingly reminded that this was actually an MGM film. If the Library had really been after a print of Capra's *Platinum Blonde*, however, then it would be on its way to them.

Sam Eckman, MGM's tough and respected man in London, answered the April letter smartly, saying that he would have to consult his associates. In 1937, he gave the identical answer. The NFL's negotiating technique was that of water dripping on stone: if they didn't get an answer, or a satisfactory one, they simply sent the same letter again a year later, with a few more titles added. By 1939, the list of films requested from MGM had grown to nineteen. For the first time they received a positive answer and the films began to flow in, although there were to be several fraught and bumpy patches in later relations with MGM. RKO answered the original letter with the comment that 'contractual obligations prohibit us at all times...from allowing copies of films to go out of our possession.' It seems that by the early 1940s, if not earlier, these problems had been sorted out. It's worth noting that by the end of 1943 prints of both *Citizen Kane* and *The Magnificent Ambersons* had actually reached the Library.

Paramount proved the most difficult company to persuade and took the most original line. The tone of their first letter suggests that they may have assumed the British Film Institute to have some influence with the government – which was far from the case.

> The three subjects you have mentioned are all *American* subjects produced in Hollywood and would therefore have no direct connection with . . . a *National* film library such as is operated by your institute. We do not want in any way to appear antagonistic to the National Film Library idea which you are developing in this country; we assume you are aware that in America similar steps have been taken. . . . If the present very undesirable quota law is ever changed, then we might find ourselves in a position to produce *British* films of such quality as would warrant their being filed with your library, but unfortunately this situation does not exist at present.

The correspondence hobbled on, with assurances from the Library that the collection was not going to be limited to British films, until in 1939 it drew a firm answer from the Paramount legal department. 'Under the terms of our agreement we must account for every print of these pictures that we have, either by destroying them and making an affidavit of their destruction or by returning them to New York.' Other companies could presumably have invoked similar agreements if they had wanted to; but only Paramount did. From the surviving records, it would seem that it was not until 1944, eight years after the original exchange of letters, that the Library began taking in Paramount films, and it isn't clear what brought about the change of heart. It was a helpful Paramount representative, however, who warned the Library that wartime distribution conditions would mean longer waits for films and a strong possibility that they would have been worked to death by the time they were handed over.

The NFL asked for 'good used' prints, which was not at all what they really wanted. Every archivist would like to get his hands on the original negative; failing that, a fine-grain master positive or, as third choice, a print in as near as possible to mint condition. But 'good used' prints (which in practice, all too often, could mean virtually worn out) were the best that the archives could hope for. These were the copies that were otherwise probably heading for destruction, and so cost the companies almost nothing, and there was no risk of arousing industry suspicions about what an archive might get up to in the way of clandestine copying, always possible if they had had better material. The quality of the prints depended not so much on official policy as on the goodwill of friendly print managers ('unsung heroes of the archive movement,' said Clyde Jeavons). Not all were friendly, though Jeavons recalled one vault manager from later years who went out of his way to help the NFA, not because he loved the Archive but because he detested his employers – if they were denying the NFA prints, he would make quite sure that they were delivered.

Many of the NFL's problems about receiving the films it asked for probably arose not from any hostility, but from the time it took for pictures to work their way through an elaborate system. The modern distribution tactic is for a nation-wide release, with those pictures clearly doomed to failure pulled out of circulation as quickly as is decently possible. In the 1930s and 40s, when almost any cinema had its guaranteed audience and twice-a-week regulars waited for the mid-week programme change, a film's release was a slow and formal business. There was the West End opening, the general release, screenings at first-run and second-run houses, and on down the line to the backstreet cinemas which put on extraordinary double bills worthy of Langlois himself. All this could take a year, even two years. The NFL would put in a request for a film early in its run, and be advised that it would have to wait. Reminders would be sent out after a year, and perhaps half the films on a company's list would duly arrive. But there were always stragglers, and if an over-stretched and chronically understaffed organisation failed to keep a check on all the separate lists it had sent out, all the films that had got left behind, then only the most conscientious companies were likely to remember their obligations. It could even happen, frustratingly, that by the time a print could have been sent the company had lost its own distribution rights and was no longer able to deliver.

The Library would have done much better if it had been able to take up the occasional opportunity to buy prints. In 1939, for instance, United Artists

Sabu in *The Drum*: Offered a brand new print for £150 in 1939, the National Film Library had to turn it down.

reported that it had no suitable used copies of the films asked for, but could supply new ones at a price. A shopping list was attached: *The Drum* (colour), £150; *Sanders of the River*, £35; *The Scarlet Pimpernel*, £40; *Roman Scandals*, £40. All in all, the Library had the chance to pick up ten brand-new prints at a total cost of less than £500, and had to turn the offer down. Unusually emboldened, Lindgren went on to make a tentative bid to acquire the original negatives on permanent loan. The answer was as firm as it was predictable. 'It would be absolutely impossible for us to obtain the approval of the producers concerned to such an arrangement.' Such cap in hand requests, with virtually no money available for purchase, showed up all the weakness of the Library's position; as its committee had forecast, it was a beggar with nothing to give, a national organisation ridiculously dependent on what amounted to the charity of an industry.

The collection, however, grew rapidly. In October 1936, the Library had 273 titles in its preservation section and 49 films available for hire. (And, in 1937, received a signal of official approval, when it was asked to keep the colour films of the Coronation procession.) By May 1938, when a second edition of the catalogue appeared, the loan section had doubled and the total holdings had passed the one million foot mark. A year later, they were already claiming two million feet in all. The BFI Governors, in May 1939, were looking to the future: 'We hope to dig a cavern safe from bombs in which this very valuable material we have acquired may be preserved.' Actually, when war broke out a few months later and the government ordered the removal of all nitrate film stores from London, temporary refuge was found in a Sussex stable, with much of Wardour Street's own movie stocks sharing the farmyard. In November 1939, Lindgren found premises at Aston Clinton, in Buckinghamshire, which was to be for years the centre for nitrate storage. For his role in conserving a national heritage, Lindgren was then being paid £265 a year.

As the Museum of Modern Art was discovering at about the same time, a very rapid rate of acquisition meant that the Library was always running to keep up with itself, with little breathing space for thinking out policies. It made no great effort to capitalise on a very fair measure of industry goodwill, to follow up Iris Barry's initiative in persuading the film companies to give a little thought to the preservation of their own past. Perhaps it took an Iris Barry to do that. And it would not, admittedly, have been easy. In the United States, there could always be the appeal to national pride, the Americans' sense of the movies as their own unique and particular creation. In France, the culture card could be played. But the general attitude of the British film trade (which does not mean that of British film-makers) was one of proud, sturdy and quite determined philistinism. They were not people, they liked to make it clear, to be bamboozled by soft talk about art and culture.

The Library kept its distance from the trade, sending out its regular form requests, but somehow conveying the impression that it found this a slightly distasteful necessity. The trade, for its part, kept its eye on the Library. In 1936, a Lumière anniversary programme was staged, including *The Birth of a Nation* and Chaplin and Mary Pickford shorts. The event was put on to raise funds for the

Library, but the *Daily Film Renter* was quick to suggest that the BFI was exploiting the work of the film industry for its own purposes. In 1939, when some films were lent to the BBC for a television programme on Chaplin, the same trade paper pounced again. 'Has the BFI any mandate from the industry which supplies its whole income to release films from its library for television or other purposes?' The reminder of where the money came from was characteristic.

All archives had to go carefully, although it may be that their caution was exaggerated. They might have issued a few more challenges to a trade press always more ready to bark than bite. There was a shaky moment, for instance, when it appeared that an RKO film which had been given to the Library might have leaked out to film societies. RKO would seem to have reacted rather more calmly than Lindgren, who fretted that 'one single instance of such an infringement might be sufficient to destroy the confidence of the film industry in the integrity of the National Film Library.'

One episode from the 1930s, though hardly central to the development of the Library, remains too central to its folklore to be ignored. It involved, of course, Harry Price. He had become friendly with R.S. Lambert, the *Listener* editor, BFI governor and member of the Library Committee, and evidently a man of a similar enquiring spirit. Price took Lambert to watch a demonstration in which an Indian walked on hot coals. Lambert then jumped at the chance to join Price in a full-scale investigation into the Talking Mongoose, which was said to be haunting a farmhouse in the Isle of Man. The Mongoose, a busy as well as a chatty creature, was reported to have been taught to communicate in English by the farmer. The two men evidently enjoyed themselves, and published a rather cheerful book, *The Haunting of Cashen's Gap*, about the escapade.

Lambert, it would seem, had become a disputatious member of the BFI's governing body, likely to try to reopen discussions if he disagreed with a decision. In one particular squabble, he crossed swords with the faction supported by Lady Levita, the BFI's token woman governor. Her husband, Sir Cecil, would seem to have had no connection with the BFI other than through his wife, but had previously befriended Lambert and felt let down. He took a BBC executive out to lunch, grumbled that Lambert's wits had been more or less addled by all the nonsense he was picking up from Price, that people prepared to consider talking to spectral mongooses were no longer fit members of the BFI board. The conversation was smartly reported back to Lambert, who brought an action for slander. He was represented by Sir Patrick Hastings, the leading advocate of the day, and was awarded damages to the handsome tune of £7,500.

The Case of the Talking Mongoose of course delighted the press and gave the nation a good deal of innocent enjoyment. Less enchanted, the Judge complained of time taken up by 'these petty squabbles between these people'. The BFI and the NFL were made to look more than foolish, as the centre of so much squabbling and absurdity. But according to Lambert's own account in his autobiography, *Ariel in All His Quality*, the case played a more significant part in the history of the BBC. The Corporation had put him under a good deal of pressure to drop his action, and it was suggested that BBC staff relations were not happy. Shortly afterwards, in November 1936, the government set up a Board of Inquiry, from whose deliberations, in due course, came the creation of a BBC staff association. The Mongoose, having enjoyed this peripheral involvement in the affairs of two national institutions, retired into obscurity, if not silence.

Another story from the 1930s, however, sums up more of the spirit of the NFL in those days, when it was looking to find an identity for itself and developing its own rules and practices. Harold Brown, still a novice, was repairing a piece of film. This would correctly mean snipping out the damaged frames and splicing the film together again, but on this occasion Brown was dealing with a diagonal tear and trying not very effectively to stick it together without losing any film. Ernest Lindgren, catching sight of this operation, was critical but kindly. 'I see,' he said, 'you were trying to preserve the frame.' And this, Brown said, was the NFL's notion of what it should be doing. Preserving the film was all very well, preserving the frame was taking things that perfectionist, essential stage further.

3

FORTRESS ARCHIVE

The film archivists would probably claim that their pioneering period did not end until 1980 or thereabouts. It took the best part of forty years, allowing for the interruption of the war, for the movement to become fully established and effective internationally, to achieve relationships with the world's film industries based on confidence rather than suspicion, and to gain recognition from governments that film preservation was necessary and worth funding. For most of the pioneering age, the history of the archive movement was also effectively the history of two men, Ernest Lindgren and Henri Langlois. They were the outsize personalities, both difficult, original and single-minded, and ideas and standards about what a film archive should do and how it should do it emerged out of their disagreements. Iris Barry took herself out of the game when she retired from MOMA in 1951. The only other possible contender was Jacques Ledoux, the very influential curator of the Royal Belgian Film Archive, but he belonged to a slightly younger generation. Lindgren and Langlois were there at the beginning: the founders, the creators, the opponents.

They were opposites in every possible way: in physique, in temperament, in their policies and attitudes and views about the role of the collections they built up. At various stages they were almost friends, as part of a movement so tiny that it could not afford dissension, wary colleagues and outright enemies. (Although the open expressions of venomous dislike were mainly on Langlois' side. Lindgren was more likely to sigh and say 'What a man' at news of the latest enormity across the Channel.) They were united only in their unremitting, totally single-minded devotion to the institutions which each had created in his own style, organisations so heavily stamped that they became mirror images of their creators' personalities. Both men died young: Lindgren (born 1910) in 1973, Langlois (born 1914) in 1977. It would not be too fanciful to suspect that they literally wore themselves out.

Photographs from the 1930s show a tall, slim Henri Langlois: 'thin as a rail', as he was described. He put on a great deal of weight with the years, so that most people's memories are of a large, usually untidy figure, defiantly overweight, whose huge bloodhound's eyes still seemed almost too large for his face. In London he enjoyed buying his suits from the High and Mighty chain of shops – the name would always have attracted him. Lindgren, by contrast, had the sort of looks that never greatly change: trim and tidy, with a hint of Scandinavian ancestry. Orson Welles would have been the obvious casting to

Ernest Lindgren

play Langlois; Max von Sydow might have had a stab at Lindgren. Langlois was voluble and dramatic; Lindgren was reserved, with a quiet, dry, if only occasional humour. Lindgren lived by rules that Langlois ignored. Langlois believed in showing films; Lindgren in preserving them.

In 1948, Lindgren wrote an article for the *Penguin Film Review* in which he drew up a kind of blueprint for the ideal archive of a still distant future. It would have to be a national undertaking: the task was altogether too big to be left to private resources. Its first duty would be to preserve films 'in perpetuity', copying the nitrate originals as necessary on to acetate, though 'in ten or fifty years time the scientists may have found an even more durable substance'. It would be housed in 'a large and attractive building in the heart of the metropolis', equipped with a 500-seat repertory cinema ('representing the last word in comfort') and a big area of exhibition space; travelling exhibitions would also be sent out. There were to be collections of books, stills and film music, facilities for students and researchers and a small lecture hall. 'One of the most active departments of my Utopian National Film Library is its...lending section.' The enterprise was to be essentially non-commercial. He even risked an estimate of the cost: something under £50,000 a year, a quarter of the expense at the time of running the British Museum, half that of the Natural History Museum.

All archivists, Lindgren suggested, carried some notion of this dream establishment in their minds 'and believe that it is worth working for, in foul weather and in fair.' Each of the existing archives (there were then something over a dozen in the world) was finding its own route towards the shared goal. MOMA had the theatre and the lending library; the Cinémathèque Française and the Prague archive were the experts when it came to exhibitions; the National Film Library had gone furthest in developing film preservation techniques.

It all sounded splendid, but the gap between the golden dream and the way the NFL actually worked and set its priorities was wide. The BFI, for instance, was very slow in acquiring somewhere to show films regularly, and the lack of a theatre did not seem greatly to concern Lindgren. It took a brilliant stroke of opportunism by the BFI director, Denis Forman, to launch the National Film Theatre. The Telekinema, a temporary structure on the Thames near Waterloo station put up for the 1951 Festival of Britain, was snapped up as the NFT's first home. But it had taken Forman to put London on an equal footing with New York and Paris. Originally, the NFT was to show archive films, which Lindgren approved; he was to become much less supportive when the theatre broadened its scope and ambitions. It was not until 1988, when the Museum of the Moving Image opened on the South Bank, that all the components of Lindgren's ideal archive were in place, though scattered over various sites in London rather than in his 'large and attractive building'. It was a major achievement, but it was an Institute achievement in which the Archive played only a secondary role. Lindgren, with his strong sense of territory, would have been very sensitive to that.

In his *Penguin Film Review* article Lindgren was already stressing the NFL's skills in preservation work: that was what interested him, what he would always see as an archive's most important task. In 1941, Harold Brown had occasion to check the same film, *The Battle of Lebbeke*, twice within a period of some six months. It had seemed in fine condition on the first run-through; six months later it had already begun to go sticky, the first sign of serious deterioration. (The first sign of decomposition is the fading of the silver image.) Lindgren consulted the experts at Kodak, who came up with a checking system for the NFL, the artificial ageing test – or accelerated ageing test, as the experts now prefer to call it. This simple chemical test, in which staff could be quickly trained and which called for no elaborate or expensive equipment, was immediately adopted. A more sophisticated variation of it, the Alizarin Red Heat Test, is still in use. Essentially, it serves as an early warning system, letting the tester know whether a film should be copied immediately or whether it can be safely returned to its shelf for a further period.

Over the years, only a relatively small number of archives have taken up this method of examining and testing films. Some, with manageably modest stocks of nitrate, prefer to check the films regularly by hand (this is the MOMA method). Some dislike the test because it does very slight damage to the film – small holes have to be punched to extract the snippets for testing. Langlois is said to have spluttered with anger at receiving a print from London 'punched full of holes – like a Metro ticket'. Some archivists, even in the 1990s, have such inadequate resources that they have to leave their collections unexplored and hope for the best. And in the 1940s, few people understood what they were taking on when they acquired films. 'They were looking at the subject matter of the film, from whatever point of view,' as Harold Brown put it. 'They didn't realise until they were brought face to face with it that there were practical things to be done. . .'

From the 1940s, the NFL began copying films on to acetate. The originals might then be scrapped. If there was still some life in them, they might even be passed on to other archives as viewing prints. This helped to create a legend, enthusiastically propagated by Langlois, that Lindgren 'hated' nitrate, that when he wasn't punching holes in it he was trying to get rid of it as quickly as possible. The reality, according to Harold Brown, was that there was so little money available for duplicating films that work was rarely done before it had to be tackled. When the nitrate originals were copied, they usually had little time to go before becoming perilously unstable. Nitrate, however, was always unpredictable: 'There were films declared unstable and duplicated, and quite a few years later they were still in a perfectly usable condition.' This is one reason why most modern archives, including the NFTVA, like to hold on to the originals for as long as they safely can.

When it came to acquiring films, Lindgren did not see a selection policy as something to be grudgingly accepted because there was no possibility of taking everything. Far from it: he believed in selectivity as a principle, would have seen little point in an omnivorous archive. General, science and history committees met regularly from the early days; a television committee was added in 1962. Lindgren expected them to be selective, and in their first years they certainly were: it took three discussions before *Gone With the Wind* was found worthy of the NFL. The committees were also a form of insurance, and any suggestion from BFI colleagues or from the Institute's government paymasters that too many films were being chosen too capriciously would never have stood a chance. The Archive was clearly trying to get the best advice available. And, as a further discipline imposed on the committees themselves, they were required to justify their choices by supplying a reason, to be duly recorded on a catalogue card. That many of these reasons looked blindingly obvious, rather silly, or like doomed efforts to compress complex thoughts into single sentences, was beside the point. The reason was, as it were, the icing on the committee cake. No other archive had a system like it: they saw it as strange, wonderful and British.

The problem was that selection did not necessarily relate very closely to acquisition. Where British films were concerned, the system must have worked rather well: the Archive has prints of 73 per cent of the British features released between 1929 and 1975. This figure looks even more remarkable when one remembers how few of the quota quickies of the 1930s (even if directed by the young Michael Powell) and the dim little B-picture thrillers of the 1950s would have passed muster with the committee at the time. The Archive is scavenging now for what it rejected then. Lindgren saw no reason to allow British films special treatment, though here the general selection committee, at least, began rather to part company with him. Increasingly, the argument became 'Well, after all, it *is* British', with the notion that if the Archive ignored the film it would certainly not be salvaged by anyone else. In the mid-70s, after Lindgren's death, it was agreed that the Archive should do officially what it was already more or less doing unofficially, and that all British features should be selected. Other countries were now looking after their own films and there was no longer the old sense of obligation on every archive to try to keep everything. The new priority was to give the home-grown product its chance.

Relations with the American companies fluctuated: placid and easy cooperation for a number of years, followed by a sudden plunge into suspicion, sometimes for no evident reason, a cutting-off of supplies, and then after months or years a return to normal service. The major difficulty for the Archive came with subtitled films, documentaries, non-theatrical productions, and this had nothing to do with ill will or inefficiency. Paradoxically, it was precisely the distributors and film-makers who were friendliest to the Archive and would most have wanted to see their films preserved who could do least about it. Spare prints could not be handed over because they didn't exist. There was even a period in the 1960s when the NFA was not taking in films produced by the BFI's own Production Fund (later Department): the production budgets were too tiny to allow even the small cost for one extra print.

Those of us who were members of the general selection committee, and sat over our sandwich lunches arguing about whether the new film by Godard or Buñuel should be elevated to category 'A' (essential to have; purchase if necessary), did not quite appreciate the general artificiality of the exercise. We didn't expect the Archive to run out to buy a print, but neither did we realise that the chance that it would *ever* have the money to buy one was remote indeed, or to quite what extent in this area the normal channels of supply were blocked.

The NFA went on sending out its formal requests, although the letter writers must have known exactly what answer to expect. George Hoellering, proprietor of the Academy Cinemas and a friend of the Archive, certainly kept patiently spelling it out to them. He did not himself own the film in question. He was sure that the overseas owner would be happy to see a print in the NFA, and he would negotiate arrangements if asked. But the print must be paid for; he was sorry that he couldn't afford to make the Archive a present of it. Impasse. Then in 1966, exceptionally, the Archive did manage to afford a print, of Robert Bresson's *Les Dames du Bois de Boulogne*. It could, just occasionally, be done. And it must have been thanks to Hoellering that Hungarofilm was persuaded to donate a print of Miklós Jancsó's *The Red and the White*. They apologised for sending only a single print. 'We are a small country, having a limited film production and a small budget.' Archives in rich countries had to be shameless about looking like scroungers off poor ones.

The main source of foreign-language films, however, had to be through exchange or barter with other archives, and the occasional acquisition of a major

Maria Casarès in Robert Bresson's *Les Dames du Bois de Boulogne*. Exceptionally, in 1966 the NFA bought a print.

collection. Early in the war, for instance, the Film Society handed over its large stock of films. Initially, this was to be for safe-keeping only. They wanted the collection to be held together as a unit and to be made available for viewing, and they expected to ask for it back after the war. They never did so, leaving the Archive with such trophies as the Film Society print of *Battleship Potemkin*. Much later, Ivor Montagu passed over the films assembled by his Progressive Film Institute – mainly Soviet and Spanish Civil War material.

Lindgren himself was one of the few early archivists who was not by temperament a collector. He seemed to have little of the passionate instinct for acquisition; there was always the suspicion that he would be prepared to let a film go rather than see it turn up, as it were, like an illegal immigrant, without the right credentials. And to the exasperation of many of his staff, he had no liking for dealing with collectors: they had almost certainly acquired their films in some improper way, they should be willing to hand them over to the Archive as a form of penance rather than a commercial deal. In any case, any archive known to be dealing with collectors would not be popular with the trade. An old archive hand suggested an imaginary encounter. 'There's someone to see you, Mr Lindgren. He says he's a collector.' 'Nonsense, send him away.' 'But he says he has the missing footage of *Greed*.' 'Oh, well, if you must. In that case you can offer him a fiver.'

Lindgren's strength was in his impartiality. He valued film for its artistic potential; he had an idea of film, a sense of its own great tradition. He appreciated film, one could say, rather more than he sometimes seemed to care for individual films. He valued non-fiction cinema as highly as fiction, though for a time he had the

42

rather strange idea that the newsreel pictures were all that counted and the commentary might be discarded. When the government after the war, and after a good deal of shilly-shallying, decided, probably on the grounds of the economy of storing films in a single place, that the Archive should act as agent for the preservation of Public Record Office films, he took that easily in his stride. In the same way, he could see the eventual move into television as a logical extension of policy. He was patiently building an institution, testing out the structures, fitting the blocks into place, even though there were never the funds that would have allowed him to think far enough ahead.

In the early 1950s, television looked much more like a threat to the archives than an opportunity. It gave the film industry – which was fighting it for audiences tooth and nail, wide-screen and 3-D – an entirely new awareness of the value of the discarded, disregarded old films. Television would take anything: there was no movie, however ancient, decrepit and poverty-stricken, which could not be sent out to earn its keep by filling a daytime or late-night programme slot. By 1956, the Museum of Modern Art was reporting that blocks of films were being withdrawn while the sale of TV rights was negotiated. Film companies might find themselves less willing to make prints available to archives; and, at the same time, television companies could put archives under pressure from the other side, trying to persuade them into doing deals. Having had one difficult industry to cope with, they now had two.

The early 1950s also saw the various problems and upheavals caused by the transfer of feature production from nitrate to acetate. In France, the government was quick off the mark. In December 1950 the so-called 'anti-nitrate' law was passed. As Richard Roud put it, this 'would make it eventually illegal to show, transport or even possess nitrate film.' Deadlines were set; only the Cinémathèque Française was effectively to be exempt. Many prints were scrapped as a consequence, but many more found their way to the Cinémathèque, deliveries being made 'in truckloads'. (In Britain, the NFA had a somewhat similar windfall in the early 1970s, after a Home Office injunction imposed much stricter conditions than hitherto for nitrate storage. A large block of Rank's nitrate holdings, some 25,000 reels, was then passed over to the Archive. Famously, the prints spent some months stacked in a car park, lashed under tarpaulins, while their fate was being negotiated.)

In the 1950s, however, there were no truckloads arriving at the NFA. Its problems, rather, were created by the gradual withdrawal of nitrate prints from circulation, particularly by the American companies. The prints represented a fire risk which no longer had to be put up with; they were out of date; new cinemas would no longer have to comply with the regulations applied to nitrate screenings. Many prints were taken out of service or junked.

The NFA went through another tricky stage in its relations with Paramount, with which dealings had generally been amicable since the first difficult years. In 1952, having heard that the company was planning to scrap prints, Lindgren put in a bid for six titles, among them Lubitsch's *Trouble in Paradise*, *One Hour with You* and *Bluebeard's Eighth Wife* and Lang's *You and Me*. He described Paramount's reaction as 'the first occasion on which we have received a flat refusal from any company'. If they could see their way to making the gesture of giving the prints to the NFA, 'it would mean very much to us as an archive, and to the people of this country.' Unmoved by this touching appeal, Paramount did not budge; in fact, the company went the other way, turning down the Archive's next routine bid for a batch of titles which included *Sunset Boulevard* ('I regret to advise you,' wrote the London representative, 'that our studio has seen fit to refuse the request') and in 1956 making a slightly ominous demand for a complete list of Paramount films held by the Archive. Even in 1959, when the NFA had heard that the British prints of *Shane* were to be withdrawn and asked for one of them, the reaction was prickly. The withdrawal of the film was 'purely a domestic matter and only of a temporary nature'. And where, in any case, had the NFA picked up its information? Such problems with companies, though not frequent, were also not rare; they were what made the Archive feel even more strongly about the case for Statutory Deposit. A failed attempt in 1956, however, left Lindgren lamenting the need to rebuild bridges with the trade after what he described as 'the most serious crisis in our history'.

It was not easy to build up a collection of films that people could hope to see. In spite of the continual stress on the importance of preservation work, the budget available for copying was never more than a few thousand pounds a year. Because films could not be copied, they could not be shown – other than on moviolas or viewing tables, to students and researchers. Lindgren would never relax the rules as originally advised by the British Kinematograph Society, to allow a screening of a film of which a viewing copy had not yet been made. Even when viewing prints existed, he did not go out of his way to make them available. The National Film Theatre programme officers, during much of the 1950s and 60s, actually felt that they could expect more cooperation, and certainly more enthusiasm, from Langlois, across the Channel, than from Lindgren, in the same building. This was the damaging side of Lindgren's often admirable stubbornness. Too readily, he came to see the Archive as a fortress under siege, threatened not only by evident enemies but by other departments of the BFI.

Over the years, the bright and expansionist archive foreseen in Lindgren's 1948 article seemed to have less and less connection with the establishment he was actually creating. If he himself still kept it as an ideal, it had to be so far back in his mind as to be almost out of sight. Lindgren would undoubtedly have hoped to become director of the BFI, but must have realised quite early on that he would always be seen as too single-minded, too exclusively an archive man. (Langlois in 1964 gloated at the news of Stanley Reed's appointment as director, seeing it as a major blow to his rival.) Disappointment, predictably, made him even more single-minded. Preservation, which had been one goal among several, began to seem the only thing that really mattered. Everything was being done in the interests of posterity, and there was no suggestion that posterity was expected to put in an appearance during the next ten years, or even the next fifty. It was impossible, in fact, to imagine the event that could trigger off the millennium for the Archive, the day when it would release the films. (In the event, although the films have not exactly been released, posterity may be said to have arrived some time during the 1980s.)

It was hard for us, his junior colleagues, to be fair to Lindgren's policies, or to see the justice of his rigorous discipline. Against his regime, which seemed to promise at best a little jam tomorrow, we could see how things looked in Paris, with Langlois spreading the jam all over the screen. Among film-makers and critics the NFA came to be seen as a kind of long-stay prison for films, a place into whose recesses they disappeared, never to be seen again. Undoubtedly, this image did a good deal of harm, and it was at many points belied by the NFA itself, always livelier, more varied, more forthcoming in its range of activities than its reputation suggested, partly because there were always staff prepared to take an independent line. The image, which reflected disappointment, was that of a man who had exhausted himself in creating the Archive, in laying down rules and principles and standards which many would come to see as the correct ones, and who no longer had the imaginative energy to explore the way forward.

Lindgren was a man of strong principles and rare obstinacy, one who did not need to have bureaucracy thrust on him but seemed to accept it naturally and to relish its detail. His memos were unfailingly lucid and elegant, though he never wrote a short one when a long one would do. One of his last major campaigns, which saw him both at his best and his most inflexible, was the bid in 1969 to achieve Statutory Deposit. This time, Dr David Kerr, a Labour MP and BFI governor, was prepared to use a private member's bill to advance the Archive's cause, giving a much better chance of success than with previous tentative efforts. The cause itself was as necessary as ever: over the years 1957-1966, it was reckoned that the Archive had asked for nearly 900 films and had received only 241.

Lindgren did not intend Statutory Deposit to become a commitment for the NFA to take in all the films made or shown in Britain. At a time when many archivists were becoming less exclusive in their ideas, he stood firmly by his old principles of selection. The Kerr bill was to achieve the best of both worlds: the Archive would have the right to ask for a print of any film screened commercially in Britain, but companies would not have to hand over the material until they were asked for it, and nothing like all the films would be asked for. Donors' rights would not be affected: films would be protected against exploitation under the new scheme as they were under the existing voluntary arrangements. It was Lindgren's view that the NFA would need a special acquisition fund to pay for the prints:

> If it were thought necessary to put some arbitrary limit on the size of the fund, it seems to me that it would be better to accept this, and to preserve with complete effectiveness a lesser number of films, rather than to continue with the present system, under which we are free to select every film considered to be of importance, but the majority of which we either do not receive at all, or receive in the form of copies not worth preserving.

The question of who was going to pay for the scheme would always be the problem. In many people's view, a rich industry ought to be ready to pay its own way, but the American companies remained opposed to the whole idea, suspicious always of the motives behind it, and could hardly have been expected cheerfully to finance its workings. And there were many areas where the industry was not rich at all – the small independent producers, hard-up documentary film-makers, distributors of subtitled films could not afford as things stood to donate prints to the Archive and would have been in serious trouble if put under an obligation to do so. The answer had to be some sort of special fund, which in effect meant money from the government.

In the event, the Kerr bill failed to achieve a second reading by a respectably narrow margin: 29 votes to 48. Jennie Lee, Britain's first Arts Minister, described it as 'a very desirable measure which the government would like to see become law in a more favourable economic climate'. There the matter rested. No government has ever opposed the scheme, in theory; none, in practice, has found the economic climate encouraging enough for it to put up the really rather small amount of money involved. In the early 1970s the suggestion was that the BFI should find the means to launch the scheme out of its existing grant. Stalemate again.

Lindgren himself, though he had prepared the ground for the bill with meticulous attention to detail, probably took quite a calm view of its failure. While it was being discussed, he became worried that Dr Kerr, his champion, had been got at by trade representatives trying to ensure that it should be restricted to films made in Britain. Perhaps the bill might have stood a better chance on those more limited terms, but Lindgren would have none of it. The NFA must preserve foreign films, just as the National Gallery must preserve foreign paintings; anything less was provincial, unimaginable. If the scheme went ahead on that basis, he argued, companies would fulfil their statutory obligations, but no more. The Americans would deliver prints of their British-made films, but there would be no more voluntary donations of the many more films made in Hollywood. And he foresaw the almost equally threatening prospect of the Archive being under an obligation to secure more British films: 'This would involve us in keeping many worthless productions of no historical interest.' If the day had been won on such unsatisfactory terms, the Archive would be given no second chance; after a lost battle, there was always the hope of reopening the fight.

In 1969, Lindgren wrote a long paper on the state of the NFA, addressed to a BFI governors' sub-committee. It is a sad document, suggesting great depths of frustration, though he might of course have felt that the more woebegone the picture, the greater the chance of winning support. From the outset, he argued, the Archive had been 'set up without material resources of any kind. . . . The poverty of this beginning, and the constant tactic of opening up an activity first and then trying to raise the money for it afterwards, have hung over the Archive ever since, hampering its development and stunting its growth.' All the machinery to do the job properly was in place, but there was such a chronic shortage of staff, money and facilities that 'full value is not being obtained even from the public money now being spent on it.'

At the existing rate of progress, he suggested that it would take in the region of 400 years to copy all the nitrate holdings. The cataloguing service was falling steadily further behind, with films being acquired three times as rapidly as the cataloguers could cope with them. He was even uneasy about the workings of the selection committees, whose standards were no longer as strict as his own and which might be getting out of hand. He was worried that the NFA was not receiving anything like the number of films it asked for, and suspected that companies were holding on to material because they planned to continue exploiting it even after copyright ran out.

Lindgren conceded that times were changing. He admitted that there might soon be a case for altering the selection system, dropping committees which were no longer needed as a defensive barrier and recognising that NFA officers were perfectly capable of making their own choices, with occasional specialist advice. (In fact, the committee system survived until the mid-1980s.) There might be a case for giving special treatment to British cinema, possibly for trying to acquire everything made in Britain. Many countries at least had the machinery to preserve their own national cinemas: pressure had been taken off the older archives, which could reorder their policies.

For a more flexible system to function, however, other archives had to be fully up to the job in hand, cooperation between them must be effective, there must be no risk that political problems could seriously hamper such cooperation, and there must be assurances that the rights owners would not try to hinder the exchange of films between archives. 'Not one of these conditions is within sight of being reached,' he concluded.

The BFI governors accepted his bleak view of the situation. The NFA was 'patently failing to achieve its objectives in almost every part of its work. Most of its problems are at root due to lack of sufficient money.' Not surprisingly, the governors did not support Lindgren's bold bid to cut the NFA adrift from the Film Institute. The Archive's position, he argued, was made even worse by the need constantly to argue its case for a few hundred pounds here and there, against other BFI departments whose demands were always likely to seem more urgent. His suggestion was independent status, the right for the Archive to go to war on its own account. But the Institute without the Archive would unquestionably be a much weakened organisation, and the Archive without the Institute might not have found independence quite the benefit Lindgren foresaw. In any case, he was left to soldier on. 'The government of the country must decide what kind of national collection it wants,' ruled the governors, disregarding the fact that this is not a matter which has ever much interested any government.

All the archive machinery was indeed in place, the rules and habits of work understood, the NFA's role on the international scene advanced. ('I don't know where FIAF might have gone without him,' said Wolfgang Klaue, former head of the East German archive.) The price had been paid in the adoption of ever more defensive attitudes, so that the Archive seemed to see itself engaged in a holding operation from which it could not break out. Lindgren was 'simply putting the films away and hoping something might eventually happen,' in David Francis's words. By the 1970s new policies could at least be envisaged, but by that time Lindgren was too tired and too ill. Three years after his death in 1973, David Francis achieved the breakthrough, launching the plan to copy all the Archive's nitrate holdings by the year 2000. But this, of course, depended on the strength in depth of the organisation Lindgren had created. Twenty years after his death, there is no question that this is still his archive.

4

THERE IS ONLY ONE LANGLOIS

Ernest Lindgren was the tortoise; Henri Langlois the hare. At the end of the day the tortoise would have to be the winner, by right as well as by the rules that apply to fables. Since his death, Lindgren's reputation has soared among his fellow professionals, in some ways because they have caught up with his concerns and can see how often he asked the right questions. For much of his career, however, Langlois was out in front, the man who gave currency to the word *cinémathèque*, not just in France but throughout the world, who made the profession of archivist fashionable – not of course by preserving films but by showing them. He created a legend, gloried in it and before the end had become its prisoner.

First and always, Langlois was a collector – of posters, costumes, stills, documents, everything connected with films as well as films themselves. 'Undeniably the greatest *private* collector of films to date and probably of all time,' Lindgren said of him, though I have added the italics. He had a truffle-hound's instinct for sniffing films out: the most loyal subscribers to the legend were prepared to believe he could literally smell them. And like most collectors he chose to display his treasures on his own terms, would otherwise prefer secrecy about just what he had and where he kept it. Scribbled lists of films were to be preferred to more orthodox records; he was said not to be above such dodges as slipping films into wrongly labelled cans. An archive, he once said, was like a bank – a Swiss bank, of course – with an obligation to maintain confidentiality about its holdings in the interests of its depositors (whether of cash or of films).

For Lindgren, the serious work began when a film entered the archive: listing, cataloguing, testing, determining its state of health, all the detail of preservation. Langlois saw it as his task to rescue films, bringing them in off the streets or away from other hazardous places into the safe-keeping of his collection. What happened to them after that concerned him much less. Having no great personal interest in work which involved administration or dull detail, he found it easy to rationalise any neglect. Cataloguing was a lifetime operation; there was nothing urgent about it. Nitrate would eventually decay, but he thought it would last longer than other people reckoned. (In this, it would seem that time may be proving him right.) In any case, a collector planning for the long-term future of his archive would also need to believe in the long-term future of the planet, and Langlois may have been rather too much of a fatalist to have that kind of confidence.

If he had received the advice about the dangers of projecting prints which the

49

Henri Langlois

BKS gave the National Film Library, he would have been temperamentally inca-
pable of taking it, even if he had been prepared to believe it. An archive which
did not show its films was, for Langlois, simply an impossibility. Although not a
man one would ever have thought of as whimsical or a sentimentalist, he could
talk whimsically about films. They were like animals, pets, condemned to the
dreariness of being locked away in the dark. Projection must be good for them,
an outing, a treat. But in saying such things, of course, he might simply have been
out to tease Lindgren and the orthodox. With Langlois, one could never be sure.

He was one of the relatively few archivists who consistently rejected any form
of selection policy. (Others have included Freddy Buache of the Cinémathèque
Suisse, a veteran Langlois ally, and Raymond Borde of the Cinémathèque de
Toulouse, an opponent of Langlois on most other points.) Choice, Langlois
argued, could become a form of censorship. He was also well aware that the one
sure thing about taste is that it changes, that any archive basing its policy on the
safe critical judgments of the day could well look very foolish to succeeding
generations. He took whatever he could get and, having taken the material in,

dumped it in whatever storage was available to him. In the 1950s, after the regulations about handling nitrate were imposed in France, the film companies unloaded vast quantities of their unwanted stocks on to the Cinémathèque. Some of this, Richard Roud suggested in *A Passion for Films*, might very well have been in a state of decay from the moment it arrived. With so much footage coming in, and no proper system of checking it, only luck would really let Langlois know the condition of his hoard.

As a collector, Langlois preferred to deal with film-makers themselves. Lindgren's form letters and Iris Barry's high-level negotiations kept dealings on an official level; Langlois chose more personal relationships where he could. He felt that the greatest asset for the Cinémathèque was the fact that film-makers trusted it – much more than they did any archive with state connections. And he believed it was essential for an archive to maintain a high profile, to be known and seen and to pursue as many public activities as possible. This was one reason for his fondness for staging exhibitions, and the care he put into them. Even a show put on in a hotel ballroom at Cannes, for a few days during the festival, would have all his trademarks of lightness, wit, cleverness and fun. And above all, of course, he put on films.

The theatres Langlois had at his disposal were not large. The one at the Cinémathèque's Avenue de Messine headquarters, from about the end of the war to the mid-50s, was virtually a screening room, with a bare fifty seats. François Truffaut, Eric Rohmer, Jacques Rivette, Jean-Luc Godard and the rest of the *Cahiers du Cinéma* team went there, and the atmosphere of a tiny club heightened the sense of excitement. This was also the immediate postwar period: a generation which had been cut off from large areas of world cinema during the war, and a new generation discovering film, were able to meet there – as they did in London at about the same time at screenings put on by the New London Film Society. In the mid-1950s, the Cinémathèque moved to a new address and gained access to a 250-seat cinema. But it was not until 1963, with the transfer to the Palais de Chaillot and greatly increased government support, that Langlois really had the space to spread himself. For many years the Cinémathèque screenings owed their influence to the concentration and quality of the audience, drawn by Langlois' dazzling programming, rather than to numbers.

In a sense, however, the first turning point for the Cinémathèque had come earlier, during the war. According to Georges Franju, quoted in *A Passion for Films*, the collection at the time the Germans marched into Paris was tiny, a mere 300 films. When the Germans left, it was nearer 3,000. This staggering increase was largely the result of the presence in Paris of Frank Hensel, head of the Reichsfilmarchiv, first president of FIAF, and now a major with the German army of occupation. Hensel apparently tipped off Langlois and Franju when films were about to be confiscated or companies were being closed down, helping them with both acquisitions and the space to store them. In a shady period, the unanswered question would have to be Hensel's motive. Was he merely acting in the spirit of FIAF, helping out a fellow archive, though doing so in improbable circumstances and going to improbable lengths? Was he, as Raymond Borde tentatively suggested in *Les Cinémathèques*, laying some of the foundations for a massive Euroarchive under Nazi control? Was he, as has also been suggested, using his FIAF post to dodge more active military service? Was he a good archivist, a good German, a good bureaucrat? For Langlois and Franju, of course, there was only one motive: to build up the collection, accepting the means.

At the same time, Langlois was sending films away from Paris, setting up caches in the houses of friends to keep his treasures safe from the Germans. (Some romantics like to believe that films may still emerge from long-forgotten hiding places, lost masterpieces which have been mouldering like so many sleeping beauties in distant chateaux.) He was also organising screenings, wherever and whenever he could. Simone Signoret claimed that her first sight of *Battleship Potemkin* was in his mother's kitchen. Not possible, said Mary Meerson, Langlois' closest collaborator, in a mood to spoil a good story: the Cinémathèque never had a 16mm print of *Potemkin*. Lotte Eisner, who had left Nazi Germany in the early 1930s and found her way to the Cinémathèque, was meanwhile dodging the Germans by passing herself off as cook at a girls' school (appropriately, under her *nom de guerre* of Escoffier). Lotte Eisner, authority on German cinema, biographer of Lang and Murnau, was also, one might say, the charming face of the Cinémathèque, Langlois' most trusted emissary on overseas errands. She was to assemble for him many of the trophies he eventually put on show at the Musée du Cinéma.

After the war, the Cinémathèque was immediately back in its stride, as was FIAF, which held its first postwar meeting in Paris in 1946. Langlois' influence over the international archive movement, already established, lasted until 1959, by which time he was also a power in a wider world. He could be extremely supportive to other archives, helping both Freddy Buache in Switzerland and Jacques Ledoux in Brussels. He had overwhelming strength of personality. And above all he had the films. From the first postwar days the archives engaged in a brisk international traffic, exchanging and lending prints. As a source of supply, the Cinémathèque Française was unmatched, and Langlois lent generously, always willing to help a cause he approved. The other archives needed his films; so did the film theatres. 'Without Langlois,' Richard Roud wrote in the *Guardian* in 1968, 'London would never have had the chance of seeing Feuillade's *Les Vampires*, Buñuel's *L'Age d'Or*, the new longer version of Stroheim's *Queen Kelly*, the complete sound-scored print of Stroheim's *The Wedding March*, many of the films of Jean Renoir, the complete print of Ophuls' *Lola Montès*, the Abel Gance retrospective.' Roud and his colleagues at the National Film Theatre received little such support from the National Film Archive.

Some archives, Langlois thought, were not at all to be trusted with prints. There was a fearful row in the early 1950s when he became convinced, rightly or wrongly, that a print of *L'Age d'Or* which had turned up in the Middle East must have originated in a copy which he had lent the BFI. Although not in some matters a man of fine scruple, Langlois prided himself on justifying the trust of the people who gave him films, the depositors in his bank. Clandestine copying

Louis Feuillade's *Les Vampires,* one of the classics Langlois rescued from obscurity.

infuriated him, and he was always suspicious that it might be going on, reluctant even to use the orthodox film transport services, as though privateers and predators might be lurking in mid-Channel. Films on loan were usually delivered by hand, with Lotte Eisner serving as messenger. She would arrive in the small *Sight and Sound* office, having travelled from France by the night ferry train, shake hands several times with everyone in sight, including stray visitors and bemused temporary typists, and settle down to a conversation which never greatly changed over the years. 'Oh, my dears, I should not be here. My publishers need me in Paris, I have my proofs to finish. But Henri insisted, so I came. . .' Henri always insisted; Lotte usually came.

On one occasion, Langlois came himself. He walked into the office, dropped his bag on a chair and began talking. His conversation, as François Truffaut described it in his preface to *A Passion for Films,* was 'a monologue revolving around a conspiracy'. He had always just seen off an enemy, attended some fateful meeting, was about to discover a lost glory of cinema. In an office much too small for him, he knocked his bag to the floor during one of his grander gestures, and out of it cascaded not a shower but a flood of small change – dimes, pennies, centimes, pesetas, cents, lire. We scuffled at his feet, picking up his haul, while he talked on, imperturbable and unembarrassed. There was to be no explanation of how he came to be carrying such a dead weight of tiny coins around with him; but this whole encounter, at once largely absurd and slightly mysterious, was characteristic of meetings with Langlois.

He lived, notoriously, in a world of plots and intrigues. He consulted astrologers and feared the worst. A note in the BFI files records a visit paid him in 1952 by Denis Forman, then director of the BFI. Langlois had been under pressure to

After the fire. Devastation at the Cinémathèque Française in the summer of 1959.

release films to French television, and was worried about the consequences of refusing. He and Mary Meerson were busily packing up some films, with the idea of shipping them out to safety in Brussels. 'I didn't know whether to laugh or cry,' wrote Forman. 'While we [at the BFI] are grappling with the real world, they live in a world which they have invented for themselves.' All the same, he added, 'Langlois' stubborn idealism has hauled FIAF at least out of the shadows of his mind into the cold outer climate where contracts are kept and money is actually paid.'

In 1959 the Cinémathèque was hit by a brutal blow, which was to have considerable repercussions. On a hot day, films had been left stacked up in an open courtyard outside its headquarters in the Rue de Courcelles. This was what many people regard as the classic situation for setting off a nitrate fire, and the films duly and disastrously burnt: the only fire, or the only one of any consequence, it was said, during Langlois' long career at the Cinémathèque. He was devastated and furious. The humiliation was the more cruel in that many of the films destroyed in the fire were awaiting transport and were the property of other archives. They had lost some irreplaceable material, but the shortcomings of the Cinémathèque's system of record-keeping, such as it was, meant that no one could exactly estimate the casualties.

It was probably not coincidental that Langlois' extraordinary decision to leave FIAF, which he had done more than anyone to create and nurture, came shortly after the fire. He had promised to bring a list of the lost films to the 1959 FIAF congress; his failure to do so, some observers thought, triggered off the chain of events which ended in his departure. The significance of the whole episode belongs to the story of FIAF, but it also had the effect of drastically worsening the already uneasy relations between Lindgren and Langlois and of damaging Langlois' credibility with his fellow archivists.

In the 1960s France had no national film archive, but the most celebrated institution of its kind in the world. This was a situation to be righted, by a government for which French prestige was bound up with the glory of its arts organisations. Langlois was supported in the move to the splendours and space of the Palais de Chaillot and given considerably more in the way of public subsidy. With the increase in funds, however, came the inevitable demand for greater accountability. The Cinémathèque was still a private concern, run by a council but ruled by its imperious secretary-general; the opportunity was there for expansion.

Langlois, however, was precisely the wrong man to be placed in such a situation. His secretive methods of operation were too engrained; he could not work easily with the administrator put in by the authorities; he suspected that the imaginary plots against him – if indeed they had been imaginary – had finally become real, and he prepared his defences accordingly. In February 1968 the council of the Cinémathèque Française, acting on the instructions of the Arts Minister, André Malraux, dismissed Langlois from his post. Pierre Barbin, who had previously directed small festivals at Tours and Annecy, was brought in to replace him. There were, of course, two views of how matters had been allowed to reach this extraordinary pass. That the government had been extremely patient and forbearing with an increasingly unworkable situation; or that the civil servants, the tidy-minded, the people who grumbled that Langlois spent too much on entertaining film stars who might give him films, and who even queried his taxi fares, had finally caught up with someone they had always seen as difficult and unmanageable. Was he still the one essential man with whom the official guardians of culture would have to live, or had he become a luxury they no longer wanted?

The Ministry must have nerved itself to its decision: it can never have been expected that Langlois would go quietly. No one, however, could have forecast the passions in the battle for the Cinémathèque, or the extent of the debts and loyalties Langlois was able to call on. The French film-makers were already mistrustful of the government, after attempts to impose a stricter, more puritanical Gaullist censorship and the banning of Jacques Rivette's *La Religieuse* (1965). Virtually every film-maker in France, from Jean Renoir to the New Wave generation who had learned their craft in the front rows at the Cinémathèque, lined up behind Langlois. Truffaut and Godard scuffled with police as they led street protests, which were joined, as Truffaut put it in Roud's *A Passion for Films*, by 'unknown faces, those of Maoist and anarchist students, some of whom were shortly to become famous'. (They included Daniel Cohn Bendit, 'Danny the Red' to the headline writers.) The Left, involving itself in a cause where the target was a soft one and the government was busy digging its own grave, turned the Cinémathèque affair into a dress rehearsal for May 1968 – when they again showed their taste for film occasions by halting the Cannes Festival.

Langlois had persuaded film-makers that their tenuous grip on immortality would be a little more secure if they gave their films to the Cinémathèque. Now the trust he had boasted of was seen to be real. Letters in support of him poured in: from Charles Chaplin, Orson Welles, Fritz Lang, Ingmar Bergman, Roberto Rossellini, Joseph Losey, Nicholas Ray. The momentum of a protest everyone wanted to join became unstoppable, with many directors making it clear that they regarded the films they had deposited in the Cinémathèque as personal gifts to Langlois, and would not hesitate to withdraw them if he was no longer there. According to Richard Roud, the last straw for the beleaguered Ministry came with the intervention of Frederick Gronich, official representative in Paris of the American producers. The major companies, the big battalions of Hollywood, were prepared to join the campaign, with some big sticks to wave. Apart from genuine admiration for Langlois, they had always much preferred dealing with individuals, and their suspicions of a potential state archive came into play.

In a situation rich in irony, the saddest touch was that André Malraux, France's most cultivated Arts minister and himself an occasional film-maker (Langlois was even credited with saving his film *Espoir*), should have dealt the blow. It was a remarkable achievement, wrote one of the French commentators, for an Arts minister to destroy a kind of museum. 'There is no shortage in France of good accountants and good administrators,' wrote Jean de Baroncelli in *Le Monde*, 'but there is only one Henri Langlois.' Malraux must have felt that he had been badly let down by his civil servants in underestimating the overwhelming public support; and Langlois himself behaved with great shrewdness, no doubt mustering his allies in private but in public saying nothing at all, aware that he could trust his friends to put his case more effectively than he could himself. The luckless Pierre Barbin disappeared from the scene. In April 1968, Langlois was reinstated, but government funding for the Cinémathèque was considerably reduced. The government had retreated, with as much grace as it could muster; any plans to establish the Cinémathèque Française as the French national archive had been abandoned. Vaults at Bois d'Arcy, near Versailles, had already been occupied by the Cinémathèque; they were to become the base for a national archive administered by the Centre National de la Cinématographie (CNC), but it was to take a very long time to recover the confidence lost in 1968.

Later that year, Iris Barry wrote to Lindgren: 'Langlois came to see me. He was very amusing, if garrulous, and really quite potty. He said that it was he who stopped the Cannes Festival and caused the students' "revolution".' Lindgren himself had been greatly incensed by all the enthusiasm for Langlois in the British press. Plaintively, he asked why everyone wrote about the Cinémathèque. Couldn't some words be spared for his own archive? And he was justifiably hurt by the implied sneer when one journalist did mention the NFA, but only to contrast what was seen as the glorious shambles of Langlois' untidy paradise with the staid and boring order that prevailed in London.

Lindgren's papers in the BFI contain the draft of a letter written at the time to the *Listener*. During the late 1960s, he pointed out, the Cinémathèque had been receiving 'more than twice as much' as the NFA in government grants. (In fact, Malraux said at the time, the Cinémathèque had been given 20 million francs over a ten-year period.) The collection amounted, Lindgren said, to about 7,000 reels of film in excellent condition – those that were in more or less regular use for screenings. There were reckoned to be some 200,000 reels in storage elsewhere, acetate and nitrate indiscriminately jumbled together, of which only some 20 per cent was believed to be in good shape. 'If more detailed examination confirms this analysis, the Cinémathèque under Langlois will not have been a saviour of the cinema's heritage . . . but one of its most massive destroyers.'

Wisely, in the circumstances, it seems that Lindgren did not send the letter. The weakness, in any case, of this damning charge was that if Langlois had not rescued the films in the first place many of them would probably have been destroyed anyhow, rather than left to take their chance in his indifferent storage conditions. During the 1968 rumpus, a group of French journalists was taken on an official tour of the Bois d'Arcy vaults, with the expectation that they would be shocked at the piles of rusty cans. But, said Langlois' supporters, he had been complaining to the government for years about damp and inadequate storage. There were two sides to most of the stories, and in 1968 Langlois' side was the only one most people wanted to hear.

After 1968, the Cinémathèque was in financial trouble – so serious at one point that Mary Meerson had to appeal to film-makers for help in paying the wage bill. Langlois, however, went ahead with his plans for the Musée du Cinéma, which opened in 1972 at the Palais de Chaillot. It was, he said, to be his permanent memorial. And it was a splendid expression of his feelings about cinema, not its chronological history but its spirit, expressed through all those witty, ingenious and enlivening associations of objects which characterised any exhibition he put on. The sense of his enthusiasm was everywhere. He had wanted a museum for years; now he had one, even if the regular operations of the Cinémathèque were left to pay the price.

I made a flying visit to Paris to report on the Museum for a magazine, and was told by Mary Meerson that Langlois intended to take me round it himself – not entirely welcome news. Mary Meerson sat near the door, knowing everything and watching everything, like those elderly women in black who dominate old-fashioned French restaurants as they crouch over the accounts. Langlois was in vigorous form, and I soon saw why. The Museum had no catalogue and no labels identifying the exhibits. The labels would come next day or next week, he said, but one knew that if he had his way they would never come. (I believe they never did.) He didn't want visitors being distracted by reading labels, or the sort of visitors who would bother to read them. More than that, as I soon realised from various sidelong looks and significant pauses, the tour was one of those tests he so enjoyed.

I hoped that I was not too shamingly displaying English ignorance, when we reached an exhibit which in a chronologically organised show would have been much nearer the beginning. It consisted of a little model ranch house, in a very French style, a toy camera and a strip of artificial grass on which were scattered some rather grubby and twisted pieces of string. It was a fair guess that this had once represented Eadweard Muybridge's famous pre-cinema experiment, when he won a bet for Governor Stanford of California by demonstrating that at one

57

point in a horse's action all four feet are off the ground at the same time. 'Oh, yes,' I said. 'Muybridge. But where's your horse?'

Langlois was extremely put out. He was obviously annoyed that his Museum had been vandalised in its first few days, even more so that this had been spotted by a visitor, and one who might be expected to report any deficiencies to the unloved British Film Institute. Shortly afterwards, he decided that he had some urgent work to attend to, and I was left to explore the rest of the show unaccompanied. Such uneasy encounters left one feeling that one was playing a minor role in a Langlois fantasy, if only as the agent from England.

Langlois spent much of the 1970s travelling backwards and forwards to America. In 1974, the American film industry signalled its high regard by awarding him an Oscar, a remarkable tribute. American admirers had also persuaded him that it might be possible to open a Cinémathèque in New York, and he spent a good deal of time looking at sites and talking about finance. Nothing came of the scheme, and inevitably the affairs of the Cinémathèque were neglected, even though he also saw the American excursions as attempts to raise money. François Truffaut, who had done more than anyone in 1968 to fight Langlois' battles, quietly left the council of the Cinémathèque. He saw the Museum as too much of an extravagance; it would have been better to spend the money on copying some of the nitrate films in the collection. Worries about the conditions in which films were being kept increased during the 1970s. Langlois' reputation was already slipping when he collapsed and died suddenly, on 12 January 1977, after a long session doing what he had always most enjoyed: programming for the Cinémathèque. He was a Falstaffian figure, outsize in both his virtues and his failings.

The legend has been fading since his death, now that the sheer impact of his personality has lost its power and a younger generation of archivists has been made aware of the damage he did by failing to protect the collection. A serious fire in 1980, three years after his death, at one of his Paris storehouses dealt another blow to his reputation: as with the 1959 fire, the full extent of the loss remained unknown – as did the scale of the collection. It was always assumed that Langlois claimed a good many more titles than he actually had. French archivists, left with an inheritance of such confusion, have only in the 1990s really come to grips with all the problems it presents. Michelle Aubert, head of the CNC archives at Bois d'Arcy, spoke of 'twenty-five wasted years', of the delay in launching a major programme for the copying of the French nitrate holdings and in achieving the kind of centralisation and secure funding that Langlois threw away in 1968, when he defended his own concept of the Cinémathèque against the chance that it might become a national institution. And this was not merely wilful: he had strong views about the morality of film archives, the need to preserve the original vision. France also was left largely outside major international developments, being represented for years at FIAF only by Raymond Borde's Cinémathèque de Toulouse.

As between Lindgren and Langlois, perhaps the fairest summing up would be that without Lindgren we might not have the confident international archive movement of today, and that without Langlois we might not have had the excitements and tensions and enthusiasms that initially propelled the movement forward. 'We are all children of Langlois,' said his old adversary Jacques Ledoux, 'even if we have rejected our father.' But Ledoux added that Langlois himself was 'the child of Iris Barry'.

5

INTERNATIONAL

Television is essentially a medium for a nation talking to and about itself, and no amount of imported programming really changes that. Cinema, from the beginning, functioned internationally. There were no language barriers, and by the time sound arrived to impose them habits were too firmly entrenched to be broken. This way of thinking internationally may be one reason that the first four film archives decided so very quickly to form their federation. They knew that they would need cooperation and exchange, and also that there could be safety in alliances. They were very much on their own. The museum and library worlds, with which they could have had affinities, would still have found film too noisy, vulgar and commercial. And as they tried to work out their rules and procedures, they had to develop relationships with the most opportunist and cut-throat of the great industries, one with no tradition of social responsibility, no habit of spending money on such things as research and development, and no love for any form of interference in its affairs by government or outside agencies. The archives could not afford to make any false moves. Among other factors, they may have felt the need to police each other.

The International Federation of Film Archives (FIAF) was founded at a meeting in Paris on 17 June 1938. Those involved were John Abbott and Iris Barry, Frank Hensel of the Reichsfilmarchiv, Henri Langlois and Olwen Vaughan, the genial enthusiast who was then secretary of the British Film Institute and who used improbably to boast of keeping the BFI's books in pencil 'because they were always changing their minds and it was easiest to rub out'. Both Iris Barry and Olwen Vaughan would appear to have had some reservations about dealing with the Nazi archive, but Langlois and Franju enthusiastically enrolled Hensel. It was the French Right which was anti-German, Franju told Richard Roud. 'The Popular Front was all for peace.' Written into the first statutes of FIAF was one clear rule: 'Rigorously excluded from the Federation are all institutions or organisations whatsoever which use their films for a commercial purpose.'

A year later the little group got together again for their second Congress. Members of FIAF have always been enthusiastic travellers, and they certainly started as they would go on; although three of the four archives were based in Europe, their meeting took place in New York. Officers were duly elected: President (Hensel), Chairman (Abbott), Secretary-General (Langlois), Treasurer (Vaughan). With that curious innocence of the real world which so often characterises novice international organisations, they planned to hold a third meeting in summer 1940, in Berlin.

The Royal Belgian Film Archive was founded in 1938, just too late for these first FIAF meetings. At the outbreak of war, according to Raymond Borde, its collection in any case consisted of precisely three films – one of them *Battleship Potemkin*. Archives were founded during the war in Switzerland and in Denmark, both at first small, private, independent creations; and in 1946 FIAF itself promptly took up again where it had left off. Paris, already established as its administrative headquarters, was the venue for the 1946 Congress.

In November 1947 Langlois wrote to Lindgren: 'I am absolutely convinced that the individual development of each cinémathèque can be effective only in relation to the development of cinémathèques throughout the world. Without international cooperation and an international understanding of the problems, we will not be able to make progress, or to overcome the inevitable crises.' It would appear that the immediate cause of this letter was a statement by the then director of the BFI, Oliver Bell, in which it seemed that he was taking an independent line on dealings with film societies. The societies, more powerful in Europe than in Britain, wanted films for their screenings; this was another area in which the archives had to tread warily. Langlois' view, which became FIAF's view, was that it would be too easy for any archive stepping out of line to cause trouble for fellow members: FIAF must work to a common set of rules and principles. Although this made sound sense, it was also striking that almost from the outset FIAF was thinking defensively.

The Federation was rapidly acquiring members. By 1948 its executive committee,

Jerzy Toeplitz and Mrs Kawakita

now minus Hensel and with Lindgren firmly established in place of Olwen Vaughan, had been expanded to include representatives from Milan, Copenhagen, São Paulo and, most notably, Warsaw. Jerzy Toeplitz, head of the Warsaw archive, was to be president of FIAF in an unbroken run from 1948 to 1971. Astute, diplomatic and cautious, he helped to ensure that lines of communication stayed open throughout the Cold War. FIAF, someone said to me, was always split between the film enthusiasts and the administrators, never between East and West. The archivists' brand of internationalism was the real thing; many of their congresses in the 1950s and 60s were held in Eastern Europe, to ensure that there would be no attendance problems because of travel restrictions. Although São Paulo was an early member, represented by P.E. Sales Gomes, the biographer of Jean Vigo, FIAF was strongly centred in Europe, with new members coming roughly equally from East and West. Iris Barry, as founder-president, kept a slightly distant eye on things. Toeplitz, in a period before fax machines and reliable international telephone systems, cannot have had much involvement in day-to-day business. Langlois as secretary-general, with FIAF's headquarters in the Cinémathèque's own building, had every opportunity to keep the organisation running as he wanted it.

FIAF had very little money, and some French financial support was obviously invaluable. Its source of income has always been the subscriptions paid by its members, and although these were kept as low as possible, to encourage new recruits, several archives had the utmost difficulty in paying their dues. Throughout FIAF's existence, the files record efforts to hold on to defaulting members, by deferred payments and other stratagems. Sometimes, however reluctantly, archives had to be cast out. Although São Paulo was one of the first postwar members, in 1963 FIAF was sadly recording that its Latin American section was temporarily no more; in spite of all the help offered, Brazil had followed Uruguay in failing to pay. Currency export problems were apparently partly to blame, and it would seem that both archives were able to linger on. Now many people, among them Mary Lea Bandy of the Museum of Modern Art Film Department, feel that Latin America has become the great area for archive growth in the 1990s. It took a long time, however, for FIAF to build up even its North American membership. In the 1950s, when Langlois could count on being re-elected each year as secretary-general, the Federation was dominated by European archives and European ideas.

Throughout this period FIAF was exploring ways to work effectively. There was exchange and barter of films between archives: the NFA always seemed to be shipping off prints of Hitchcock's *Blackmail*, then its trump card in the exchange business. Richer archives set up a pool of spare prints to help out poorer ones, although Lindgren thought that the smaller archives, with little of their own worth exchanging, were inclined to use the service merely as a lending library. He was also scathing about a 'stamp collector mentality', arguing that too many archives were swapping prints in poor condition, building up collections of indifferent material rather than making the effort of going for the best available. Most archives, however, were 'so young and undeveloped and inadequately financed that my proposals must have seemed beyond their immediate reach.'

The more ambitious plans for international cooperation mainly fell apart, for lack of resources or of will. There was a good deal of talk, but never much more than talk, about setting up an international bureau of film historical research. There were plans for each archive to concentrate its attentions on some particular area of cinema. In one such venture, the Cinémathèque Suisse volunteered to build up an international library of film books at its Lausanne headquarters, the notion being that other archives would feed it with spare copies. In 1955 they reported, rather forlornly, that no books had been received – even willing donors had no copies to send. It was, as Toeplitz was later to describe it, the archives' era of improvisation; and of impoverishment.

In 1959 Henri Langlois walked out of the FIAF annual congress, which that year took place in Stockholm. Elderly archivists still recall the occasion, as though they had been present at some kind of unprecedented natural disaster. Although Lindgren cannot be regarded as an unbiased witness where Langlois was concerned, his account of the whole perplexing series of events is lucid, plausible, and agrees with others on all points that can be checked.

Langlois arrived in Stockholm in a mood to make trouble, knowing that he would be expected to account for the losses from the fire at Rue de Courcelles. It was partly to distract attention from this potential embarrassment, Lindgren suggested, that he launched an attack on Jacques Ledoux, the Belgian archivist, for breaking the FIAF rule that archive should speak only unto archive. This regulation, designed to stop archives poaching on each other's preserves, meant that in any dealings with, for instance, American distributors in Paris, Ledoux should have used Langlois as an intermediary. Not all archivists, it would seem, are absolutely scrupulous about keeping to all rules. But Ledoux, who had not intended to attend the Stockholm meeting, took the accusation seriously enough to rush there to defend himself. Langlois had left his evidence behind in Paris. The matter, it was agreed, must be shelved. And it was in this already acrimonious atmosphere that FIAF proceeded to its annual elections. Langlois was confirmed, as usual, as secretary-general. He waited until Ledoux was voted on to the executive committee, muttered that he couldn't possibly work with 'such a person', gathered his papers together in the most effectively theatrical way and stalked out. He never went back.

His motives were never entirely clear. Was it an angry gesture from which he later found it impossible to back down? Was his distrust of Jacques Ledoux so great? Did he feel that FIAF was no longer the original association of a few like-minded enthusiasts but an organisation he found increasingly unsympathetic, gathering round itself the usual paraphernalia of international bureaucracy? Did he think he could divide it and still conquer it? A book published in 1992, with material not available to Langlois' biographers, does not answer the questions, but it does provide revealing insights into the always devious workings of his mind.

Le Dragon et l'Alouette is a collection of letters, the record of a correspondence lasting thirty years between Langlois and Maria Adriana Prolo, founder of the Museo Nazionale del Cinema in Turin. Meticulously edited and annotated by Sergio Toffetti, the book is a fascinating piece of film history in its own right, the record of a friendship between two people obsessed with their work and their battles with the bureaucrats and the administrators. Maria Adriana Prolo was one of those impossibly tenacious people who in the end, at whatever cost to themselves and probably to most of those around them, manage to achieve something at least of their dreams. She set out in 1941, without aid or encouragement, to launch a film museum. By 1948, when she was well on the way in her perennial struggle to find funds and secure premises, she had encountered Langlois. He described her disparagingly in a letter: 'A little provincial who knows what she wants. And what she wants is a position, a Museum, the approval of Turin...' But he took her up, confided in her, chivvied, patronised, bullied, encouraged and supported her for the next thirty years.

Prolo, evidently a charming woman but in her letters a distinctly woebegone one, needed a good deal of encouragement. In 1955: 'The absurdity of the work that we do, in giving our whole life, our means, our best years, happiness, even health, for a chimera... I am in the depths of despair.' In 1958: 'If it were not for l'esprit FIAF I would give it all up.' In the same year, to Lotte Eisner: 'Dear Lotte, I have chosen my prison.' One can appreciate the value of FIAF's brand of comradeship to someone who felt so isolated in her own work, at a time when launching a film museum had to be an act of blind determination. But Prolo was a battler, if often a despondent one, and the kind of ally Langlois appreciated.

The impression given by Langlois' post-1959 letters is not so much that he had left FIAF, however it may have looked to other people, but that he thought FIAF had left him – and that he could get it back. Some old associates followed him out: Freddy Buache of the Cinémathèque Suisse; James Card, of Eastman House in Rochester, New York; Mrs Kawakita, of the Japan Film Library; and of course the trusty Maria Adriana Prolo herself. In January 1960 Langlois assured her that there were now two FIAFs – the 'legal one', his one, based as always at the Cinémathèque, and the 'other one'. In February 1960 he was 'worried about FIAF', and considered opening records which would reveal infringements of its statutes and of copyright. 'But there are things a gentleman [in English] doesn't do.' In January 1962 the fight still dragged on. 'FIAF is dead,' he wrote to Prolo. Soon its 'decomposition' would become evident.

The events that followed his departure became increasingly comical, though FIAF could hardly be blamed for failing to see a funny side to them. The comfortable arrangements whereby FIAF's quarters were in the Cinémathèque building became a good deal less comfortable. When FIAF suspected that its mail was being delayed and tampered with, it was agreed that the solution likely to cause the least fuss was to operate from a post-office box address. (If there was interference with the mail, it was probably not Langlois' own doing: it certainly was not his style.) Marion Michelle, executive secretary of FIAF and the particular bête noire of Langlois and Prolo, who spitefully nicknamed her 'Madame Mirlifiore' and saw her as machinator in chief, was duly instructed to set up the new postal arrangements. She found this impossible: FIAF, it turned out, had never been registered by Langlòis with the French authorities, and had existed happily in France for many years without knowing that it had no legal status there.

The Federation moved out of the Cinémathèque building to another address in Paris, a departure which was too pragmatic for Langlois, bewildering him almost as much as it infuriated him. His argument, throughout these squabbles, was a peculiarly legalistic one. By FIAF's own rules, all its activities in France had to be conducted through the Cinémathèque, as its representative. Therefore any action which did not directly involve the Cinémathèque had to be invalid. This, he thought, would in the long run secure his own position. Meanwhile he would keep them guessing. 'Silence, silence in the present situation is the greatest strength,' he wrote to Prolo in July 1960. 'Are we in FIAF or are we outside it? Nobody knows. Am I or am I not a member of the executive committee? Nobody knows.' He even reappeared abruptly and briefly in his secretary-general role, apparently for the sole purpose of sacking Marion Michelle – which, it turned out, he did not have the authority to do.

In all these protracted manoeuvres, FIAF showed extreme patience, reluctant to take the final step of replacing Langlois. Eventually, he brought matters rather absurdly to a head. He retaliated against FIAF's move from the Cinémathèque by obtaining a sequestration order, ensuring that the Federation's possessions, including its papers and records, remained locked away out of reach in its former office. And he registered a French organisation with objectives virtually identical to those of FIAF, though with no members except himself and one or two of the Cinémathèque staff. This had the effect of so bemusing the authorities that FIAF was unable to regularise its own position in France. These were wrecker tactics, Langlois at his most mischievously inventive, and an expression of the intense dislike he felt for former colleagues, now seen as malevolent intriguers. Jerzy Toeplitz, Ernest Lindgren and Marion Michelle were the hated trio. 'It's marvellous,' he wrote to Prolo, 'to feel free of these vampires.'

Thick files in both Brussels and London record the rather dreary progress of the legal action which FIAF felt constrained to bring, against Langlois personally. It dragged on for several years, eventually being settled in a rather half-hearted way out of court, though it was not until 1978 that FIAF managed to catch up with its incarcerated property. And in 1964, despite determined and optimistic efforts to stay in France, FIAF was forced to pack its bags. French law required that any resident international organisation should have a French representative. There was some notion that FIAF might move to London, but this, it was thought, would look too much like Lindgren's revenge, 'a continuation of the Hundred Years War'. The Federation found its new home in Brussels. Jacques Ledoux was already established as secretary-general, a small, brisk, short-sighted man, the owl replacing the dragon. Order, of a kind, returned.

For Lindgren, the issue had essentially been whether FIAF should function as a democratic organisation or allow Langlois to dictate and dominate. If Langlois split the Federation, he was prepared to leave it. To Iris Barry, it seemed that

Langlois had worked himself into an impossible position: 'The reasonable course would have been to withdraw the [original] charge, but this his *amour propre* and his personal hostility to Ledoux refuse to allow him to do.' 'I gather that the Langlois lawsuit drags on,' she wrote later to Lindgren in an undated letter, 'and that he is up to no good as usual. What a bore and what a pity that we didn't have a showdown with him long ago.'

The whole affair, undoubtedly, rocked FIAF to its foundations. Langlois reckoned that it could not possibly do without him, and in some ways he was right. The Cinémathèque was a major source of film supply for other archives. In 1962, FIAF reluctantly but inevitably decided to suspend it from membership, as a prelude to expulsion: 'It is no longer possible for FIAF to tolerate within its membership an archive which for two and a half years has done everything possible to bring harm to the Federation and its members.' There were to be no more dealings over films, an embargo which had to be costly and which might prove unworkable.

FIAF, however, proved more grown up and resilient than Langlois had expected: in effect, it had become an organisation, rather than a collection of individuals. In 1960 the membership gave the committee overwhelming support for their handling of the affair, and under pressure the Federation continued to hold together. Gradually, Langlois' allies went back, in Maria Adriana Prolo's case sadly and shamefacedly. In the early 1970s she tried to persuade FIAF to invite Langlois to rejoin. But would he want it, asked Ledoux. In fact, the Cinémathèque Française returned to FIAF as an observer (something less than a full member) in 1982, after the film-maker Costa-Gavras had been appointed as its president. It was only reinstated as a member in 1991.

The ban on dealings with the Cinémathèque lasted only a couple of years or so. Before it came into force, but at the height of the rumpus, a letter from Langlois to James Quinn, director of the BFI, is a particularly fine example of his delicate mischief-making. Langlois needed films from the NFA for a Hitchcock season he was putting on in Paris, and thought that Lindgren was showing no alacrity in shipping them across the Channel. This was quite possible, though Lindgren's defence, that Langlois had never bothered to tell him when the films would be needed, was just as plausible. It would be embarrassing, Langlois wrote to Quinn, if the British ambassador, or the ambassador's wife, or other senior staff from the embassy, turned up for a film and had to be told that it was not on the screen because it had not yet left London. This, however, would be a matter for the British among themselves. He was not going to enjoy having to give the same answer to M. Hitchcock... Only Langlois could have devised a threat based on the entirely improbable notion that the Paris embassy would be turning out in force for a Hitchcock retrospective.

The Federation may have surprised itself at the relative ease with which it adapted to life without Langlois. Improvisation, it was decided, was to be no more: the future lay with science and research. A preservation commission was set up to advise members on techniques and try to establish standards, followed by commissions dealing with documentation, cataloguing, questions of film copyright (this one later disbanded) and, although not until the 1990s, programming. It is through these commissions that FIAF has done much of its most useful work, bringing into play the knowledge of its experts and ensuring that members are kept in touch with the latest developments in areas of considerable technical complexity.

In 1961, a paper of recommendations about archive attitudes to television showed how much of FIAF's thinking was still governed by apprehension about possible industry reprisals. As long as the film companies regarded television as 'a serious and dangerous form of competition', which they clearly did, the archives would have to be extremely circumspect in their dealings with it – they must, in other words, avoid any suspicion that they might be trading with the enemy. 'It is essential that film archives should consider all existing forms of television, without exception, as being commercial or para-commercial activities potentially dangerous to the welfare of the archive, by reason of the fact that in one single irrevocable transmission a film can be shown not merely to a few hundred but to many millions of people.' The many millions might, of course, include people who had rights in the film, even those suddenly reminded of its existence. Television had killed the old exclusivity: films which the archives had jealously guarded, which they had treated as unique, rarities to be shown only to researchers on their own premises or at best at small cinemas under their control, were finally out in the open. It was a radical change.

In 1964, Lindgren produced a paper on the archives then in existence. His premier league, as it were, consisted of the three survivors from the earliest days – London, Paris and New York – plus the archives of Rome, Moscow, Prague and East Germany. There were by then nineteen other archives which he rated as of medium importance, and a further fourteen smaller ones. The movement was still predominantly European, although by the mid-1960s FIAF could already boast that it had members in every continent except Africa south of the Sahara. There were efforts, supported by UNESCO, to persuade a leading African film-making country, such as Senegal, to establish an archive. Over the years further attempts were made, but in terms of a major initiative FIAF regards Africa as its one signal failure. (There are a few very small archives, including one in Angola; the South African archive departed from FIAF during the apartheid years.) FIAF's greatest success in such ventures was its encouragement and support for the Bangkok archive, founded in 1984. The Swedish Film Institute, under its energetic director Anna-Lena Wibom, was much involved with the Bangkok project, although in general it was the East German and Soviet archives which made the running in schemes for Third World expansion. Others were less enthusiastic, feeling that FIAF was trying too hard to perform as a 'mini UNESCO'.

Gosfilmofond, the mighty Russian archive, which at one time boasted a staff of more than 500, had been founded in 1948, though films had been kept in the Soviet Union long before that. No other country has been able to hold on to so large a percentage of its national production, because no other country had a state film industry with such a long and unbroken record. Former Soviet republics, particularly those with their own solid film-making traditions, such as Georgia

International excursions. At Vence in the South of France, 1953. Left to right: Jan van der Vaal (Amsterdam), Ernest Lindgren (London), Hans Wilhelm Lavies (Wiesbaden), Ove Brusendorff (Copenhagen), Mary Meerson (Paris).

and Ukraine, also kept their own films, mistrustful of Moscow even before the break-up of the Soviet Union. And while most West European countries were still coming to terms with the existence of film archives, and state aid was being doled out in miserly dribs and drabs, the 1950s and 60s were the great growth period for the archives of Eastern Europe. Research centres were attached to archives; they had their secure place in the state cinema system. In the late 1950s a document was produced on staffing. Although the actual figures were probably unreliable, the pattern was clear enough: the archives in Warsaw, Budapest and Belgrade each had some 25–30 staff: both the NFA and MOMA listed twelve, Brussels six and Stockholm four.

Funding gradually became less generous for these archives. Eventually the move towards privatisation in Eastern Europe, if it did not threaten their existence, cut back on their staffing and research work. When in the 1970s, for instance, it had looked as though FIAF might have to shut down one of its regular activities, the publication of an international index to film periodicals, the Bulgarian archive offered to pick up the bill to keep the service running. But it was also the Bulgarian archive which in 1992 sent out a sort of sos message in the FIAF Bulletin: 'The National Film Archive of Bulgaria has only one aim now – to survive physically.'

The great film-making nations of Asia have on the whole shown no major concern about preserving their cinematic history. The Indian archive at Poona, small and modestly funded by the state, has little chance of coping in any adequate way with the output of the world's most prolific and disorganised film industry. And India has a lost heritage which is likely to remain lost, partly because the original negatives were so often used as printing material and so damaged or

At Mo i Rana in the Arctic Circle, 1993. Left to right: Vladimir Opêla (Prague), Gian Lucca Farinelli and Vittorio Boarini (Bologna), Clyde Jeavons (London). Front: José Manuel Costa (Lisbon).

sacrificed. Hong Kong, which was quick to attach itself to the international film festival circuit, only began in the early 1990s to think about an archive. The Chinese archive in Beijing has of course been subject to enough constraints since it was set up in 1958. In 1988, it recorded that it held some 6,000 features, a modest total for a major nation. But it is Japan, which shows so much regard for its history in most areas of national life, that has probably the most dismal record when it comes to preservation of its films. Most of the nitrate prints and negatives were simply thrown away, and there has been little public support for film preservation in a country where all the concentration has been on advances in electronic image-making.

Mrs Kawakita of the Japan Film Library was one of those who left FIAF in Langlois' wake; the film collection was in any case a small one, although her work in publicising Japanese films throughout the world was of immeasurable importance. In 1992 the Japan Film Centre was in the process of joining FIAF – a somewhat slow business because prospective members serve a kind of probationary period as observers, to ensure that they are able to follow FIAF's many rules. In a slightly woebegone speech at the 1992 Pordenone festival, the Japanese representative could only bewail the 'cultural crimes' of previous generations and promise a fresh start. A mere 4 per cent or less of all Japanese films made before 1945 are known to have survived – and some of those only thanks to the American occupation forces, who confiscated films immediately after the war and later returned them. Much of the destruction of Japan's film history has been blamed on earthquakes and air raids; excuses rather than reasons for a lamentable record, thought the Film Centre spokesman. Meanwhile the Japanese are trawling other countries in the hope of rediscovering some of their own lost past,

69

making discoveries as far afield as Brazil. And, ironically, they brought to Pordenone a collection of rare *European* silent films, assembled by an enthusiast in Japan during the 1920s. Survival takes strange forms, in strange places.

As FIAF expanded during the 1960s and 70s it had to come to terms with its own future, the question of how exclusive it could afford to be. Both Lindgren and Ledoux took a purist line: there were suggestions that new archives should be independent and autonomous, that they should not be part of any other concern, such as a film institute, which might in some of its activities have been infiltrated by the profit motive. After Lindgren's death, even the status of the NFA came briefly into question, with Ledoux noting that it had been 'even less autonomous than we thought'. But FIAF had either to remain a small, exclusive club or to reckon with a new kind of establishment, archives which had to show films to survive, which had to function as national film centres, and which in many cases had not much of a cinematic past to worry about, so that their thoughts were not dominated by nitrate and the need to preserve it.

All archives, even those most concentrated on preservation work, have also wanted to show their films; they could hardly have done otherwise. Ernest Lindgren, for all his passion for preservation, spoke a great deal about the need for screenings. It was his temperament rather than his principles which made it seem that he felt the proper place for a film was in its can rather than on a screen. But the older archives existed in countries where there were art houses and film societies, established routes to the screening of subtitled, offbeat or not evidently commercial films. Some of the newer archives had to fill all those roles; and to rely on screenings for the income to support whatever preservation activities they could manage. They were, in Lindgren's view, little more than 'cine clubs with film collections'.

Wolfgang Klaue, former director of the East German archive in Berlin, and one of the major enthusiasts for the drive to try to increase FIAF's membership in the Third World, told me that he saw FIAF's 1969 Congress as the time when the clash of generations became evident. Younger archivists had to be steered towards the need to preserve films; it could no longer be assumed that they accepted it automatically. In many cases they would have been hard-pressed to find adequate resources for the most expensive activity, and the one least likely to attract public support. The Federation took the route towards expansion, though without relaxing its non-commercial principles. Have some archives exploited their collections? Yes, probably, Wolfgang Klaue told me. But although archives have been removed from FIAF for failing to keep up their subscription payments, it would seem that there is no record of dismissal for bad behaviour.

The gap between the stronger and weaker archives became evident in the late 1960s and early 70s, during protracted negotiations between FIAF and the all too similarly initialled FIAPF, the International Federation of Film Producers. The notion was that the archives' position in relation to the rights holders should be regularised. In practice, however, it turned out that FIAPF was not yet in a mood to concede much, if anything. The producers' main insistence was that all films deposited in an archive remained the property of the film-makers, with a suggestion that this arrangement might be extended even after a film's copyright had expired, and that the producers had the right at any time to withdraw any films. Lindgren, characteristically, reacted with splendid hauteur: 'The British government does not give us money to provide what could be free temporary storage at the public's expense.' The producers' underlying assumption, he thought, was the insulting one that 'all archives were irresponsible and untrustworthy, potential criminals and black marketeers, whose activities had to be policed in every clause.' He was willing to concede the producer's right to withdraw a film 'if the archive has misbehaved itself, but not otherwise'. And the National Film Archive, of course, had never misbehaved.

In the long run, FIAF and FIAPF never managed to come effectively to terms. The archives less confident of their position signed the agreement, feeling that they had no choice. The stronger ones held out and refused to sign. It was virtually the last time that the archives needed to take such a stand: industry cooperation, though slow in coming, had arrived generally by the 1980s, though producers still can, and do, remove their films from archives.

All the same, at the 1992 FIAF Congress in Montevideo, Wolfgang Klaue felt it necessary to draw attention to the whole question of the rights and duties of archives, and the still largely unresolved complexities of their legal position. What, he asked, was FIAF's official attitude to Statutory Deposit? Some archives have it, some don't, and it has been consistently opposed by the American producers in particular, who remain suspicious of some form of state intervention. (Though it could be said that the United States has its own form of deposit system, through the need to register films with the Library of Congress for copyright.) Have archives in fact the right they assume to make copies of films, even for preservation purposes? Have they the right to destroy prints deposited with them, even when these have reached the end of their life and become dangerous? Have they the right to make duplicate prints for limited screenings, and do such prints then remain the archive's own property? What precisely is the archives' understanding of film copyright? And so on.

These were the kind of basic questions being discussed in the 1970s by the FIAF copyright commission, which was disbanded because it was felt that there was too much variation in copyright law between countries for it to go beyond the point it had reached. Possibly such questions were raised again in the 1990s because FIAF had recently acquired a programming commission, recognition in effect that programming had become too important an activity to be left to individual members. Perhaps the intention was to remind younger archivists of the need still to go carefully, not to assume rights which may be permitted in practice but which are not adequately defined internationally in law. Film copyright has in any case become much more difficult to enforce since video opened up the possibility for almost anyone to copy almost anything; which does not mean that copyright holders are necessarily less determined to enforce their rights where they can.

The archives' position on all these matters was much strengthened by a UNESCO recommendation of 1980 for the safeguarding and preservation of moving images, which called for measures for the physical protection of the 'moving image heritage' and for access 'as far as possible' to 'works and inform-ation sources. . .which are acquired, safeguarded and preserved by public and private non-profit-making institutions.' Most significantly, the recommend-ation invited member states to introduce some form of statutory deposit for 'any part or all of their country's national production', although of course leaving open the whole problematic question of how this should be financed. It was also suggested that foreign producers should be encouraged to continue the system of depositing voluntarily 'a copy of moving images of the highest archival quality, subject to all the rights there in'.

Archives, governments and UNESCO do not move rapidly. It had taken UNESCO a long time to work out its recommendation, which embodied many though by no means all the arguments the archives had been putting forward for years. The recognition of the case for statutory deposit was certainly significant, though more than ten years after the recommendation it had yet to be accepted and implemented by many governments, including that of Great Britain. An official recommendation, in the long run, comes down to no more than a recommendation, an assurance of status for the archives, assuming that in 1980 that sort of assurance was still needed.

In 1977, Jacques Ledoux had resigned from his post as FIAF's secretary-general. Officially, he spoke of 'incidents which lead me to state categorically that the Federation is no longer as united as it has been in the past.' Unofficially, he wrote to the NFA of the increasing influence of political considerations. 'I was no longer able to control these conflicts and all I could do was count the blows on both sides.' In effect, Langlois, Lindgren and Ledoux all had their own notions of FIAF and of the kind of archives that should properly be encouraged; and Ledoux, though considerably more of a diplomat, was hardly more of a democrat than Langlois. It was inevitable that the Federation should outgrow its creators; and since 1977 there have been several changes of secretary-general, a move away from the situation in which the office became a long-term power base for an individual.

To celebrate its fiftieth birthday, in 1988, FIAF published an anniversary volume, including a list of its members and observers, with details of their film holdings. This showed not merely the growth of the organisation, but differ-ences in size and scale which must make it increasingly difficult for the Federa-tion to speak, as some would like it to, with a single voice. The largest were the National Film Archive, with 30,000 features, 30,000 short films and 40,000 newsreels; the Bois d'Arcy archives of the Centre National de la Cinématographie (France's national archive since 1968), with 32,000 features and 63,000 shorts; Gosfilmofond, with 22,600 features and 25,400 shorts; and the two biggest American archives, the Library of Congress Motion Picture, Broadcasting and Recorded Sound Division, with 25,000 features and 55,000 shorts, and the UCLA Film and Television Archive, with 30,000 features and long television programmes and 25,000 shorts and short TV programmes. (MOMA's Department of Film, for all its seniority, also retained its exclusivity,

Jacques Ledoux. Courtesy of Jean-Michel Vlaeminckx.

with a mere 4,000 features.) The two major American archives are both in special positions: UCLA on Hollywood's doorstep, the home of collections from many of the major studios and of the Hearst Newsreels Library; the Library of Congress as the place where a film must be registered in the United States to establish copyright. At the other end of the scale came some engagingly tiny archives: Iceland, with 50 features and 950 shorts; Ecuador, with 48 features and 87 shorts; and the Filmoteca Vaticana, the Vatican archive, with 50 features and 1,150 shorts.

For most of the last two decades FIAF seems to have been asking the same kind of questions about its role, while developing the detailed work of its commissions. Should it reflect the range and different interests of its members, and to what extent; should it function as a driving force or as a co-ordinating centre? These are issues which must regularly engage any international organisation, but for FIAF the questions are complicated by resources barely adequate to even quite modest ambitions.

In many ways, the Federation is a congenially democratic organisation, small enough for most of its members to be on first-name terms and aware of the details of one another's problems, cheerfully extending a kind of family tolerance to elderly members who evidently bring out some well-worn prejudices for regular congress airings. But although in principle all archives are equal, the practice is bound to be somewhat different. Archives which struggle to meet their subscription charges are unlikely to be able to afford the travel FIAF expects of its busiest members – attendance at the annual congresses, the executive committee and commission meetings. The purpose of the congresses is to bring members usefully together, but some of the smaller archives are hardly ever seen and keep in touch only by sending in an annual progress report. The 1992 Montevideo Congress brought out a flock of Latin American archivists, which was plainly the intention, but few of them would probably have been able to follow FIAF to its 1993 rendezvous, a new archiving complex in Norway, in the Arctic Circle. The older and richer archives, which in effect means those from Europe and North America, take the lead as they always have done; though efforts are made, said Eva Orbanz, the present secretary-general, to ensure that there are at least Latin American representatives on the commissions.

The Federation has so little money from its subscription income that it has never been able to afford the luxury, if it's still a luxury, of public relations. Its image, one could say, is not so much low-key as almost non-existent, beyond the people who have direct dealings with it. The central organisation cannot afford to finance the summer schools which provide technical training for young archivists from the Far East and elsewhere. (Moral encouragement, advice and training are seen as FIAF's best aid to its younger members.) The East German archive supported these training programmes while it had the resources; in 1992 the National Film Archive put on an intensive three-week course, but with no assurance that it could be repeated. At the time in the 1990s when archives have come under the heaviest pressure not only to do more but to be seen to be doing it, neither individual members nor FIAF itself have much opportunity for expansion. It seemed appropriate enough that the 1992 congress should find itself discussing the latest technological developments in a building equipped with nothing more advanced than a slide projector.

In British Film Institute circles, the Federation did at one time have a reputation, of a somewhat bogeyman kind. 'I don't think that FIAF is going to like that,' someone would say, and quite often an argument would be stopped in its tracks. This particular ghost was effectively laid by a visit to FIAF's agreeable but very unassuming office in a quiet residential district of Brussels, where a part-time executive secretary, with two part-time aides, conducts the day-to-day business. Brigitte van der Elst, who joined FIAF in 1971, is a model of experienced calm and assurance, but there is none of the front and flash, the corporate image that international organisations like to boast.

Some members would like to see structural changes that would strengthen the central mechanism: a full-time secretariat, with more authority to take decisions on its own account; a new style of subscription, whereby the archives with the largest budgets would pay a proportionately greater share; perhaps biennial congresses, to encourage a wider spread of attendance. But one thing that one learns about the archive movement is that it is not in the habit of acting quickly, perhaps least of all in matters that concern itself. In any case, an organisation which owes its undoubted character to its dependence on the initiative of its members might not want to change that.

One significant development has been the shift to a far greater openness in relations between archives ('very important, and very new,' said Michelle Aubert). It is not merely that they talk to each other, but that they exchange serious information. Old traditions of secrecy, once so powerful, are said by many to have been virtually abandoned. An archive thinking of restoring a film, for instance, may well use the FIAF Bulletin to advertise its intentions and enlist help from colleagues who might have additional material or a different version of the film. If this might seem to outsiders a fairly basic level of co-operation, it is a huge advance on the days when almost all archives preferred to keep information about what films they had to themselves. (And were even encouraged in this by the producers, who could more easily deny the existence of a print; Langlois was a great believer in never telling one company what another had given.) The reason for the difference in attitude is basically that the archives are no longer scared; the surprising thing is that it took them so long to reach this point.

The archivist who takes a particularly firm line on such questions is Michelle Aubert, head of the Archives of the Centre National de la Cinématographie (CNC). She worked for many years at the NFA in London, indoctrinated in Lindgrenism, accustomed to an arm's length relationship with the British film industry. Returning to France, she found herself in charge of an archive controlled by the official organisation which deals with all film industry matters – and which, incidentally, produces the most enviably thorough cinema statistics. She felt she was in a position to cast aside the old damaging attitudes of defensiveness. She was part of the 'family' of the CNC, and there was nothing to stop her using the family connections. In relations with the industry, she would listen to what it wanted and what it expected from an archive, bearing in mind the film-makers' own growing awareness of the need to safeguard their films. 'We work with the grain of the industry, not against the grain.' The CNC Archive may be in a rare position to benefit from such relationships, thanks to its combination of easy access to the film trade and a stake in a government policy laid down not merely for the CNC as a whole but for its component parts. But archives which find it easy to work with the industry have an undoubted advantage, which seems likely to be increasingly felt.

This may be for the future. Meanwhile, it's enough that the archives do more readily share their information, though they still have to ask for it. There has been no general enthusiasm for any notion of archives publishing complete lists of all their holdings, still less for a computerised FIAF database. It may come, Eva

Orbanz told me, but she did not see it as a pressing need. Long before computers, Lindgren suggested some such plan, but he was so conscious of the probity of the NFA that he was never apprehensive about the publication of open lists. Some archivists, however confident in their new attitudes, might still think twice before going so far, still hesitate before admitting just what they have and just how some films were acquired.

Apart from coming together in a general way through FIAF, the archives have also organised themselves into regional groups, including an alignment of Latin American archives. The North American archivists, Mary Lea Bandy said, used to meet mainly at FIAF congresses; now they also get together regularly on their home ground to discuss problems and policies. In Europe, the minds of the archivists have been sharpened and concentrated by the prospect of cash from the LUMIERE project, a part of the European Union's MEDIA programme.

The MEDIA schemes have dealt mainly with various forms of aid to the industry – script development, subtitling, help with distribution for more specialised films, and so on. The countries of the EU share out the administration of the schemes, with LUMIERE going to Portugal. José Manuel Costa of the Portuguese archive presides over a committee of European archivists, with modest EU funds to allocate to specific undertakings. Money is available for film restoration schemes on which two or more EU archives cooperate. (Early ventures included *L'Atlantide*, to be worked on by the French and the Dutch, with a grant of 20,000 Ecus; Joe May's *The Indian Tomb*, bringing together two German archives, the French CNC Archive and 24,700 Ecus; and the work of the pioneer film-maker Alfred Machin, a collaboration between the French, Belgian, Dutch and British archives.) There is also EU support for the training of archivists, for the search for lost European films, and for a very ambitious plan indeed – the compilation of a complete European filmography.

Somewhat optimistically, it is intended that this international effort should be completed by 1995, the cinema's centenary year. The notion is that all films will be listed from the earliest silent days until 1915, and all features from that date to the present, the whole thing to be of course computerised. The data to be recorded will be fairly basic, without including anything like full film credits; and even that is going to take some assembling, not least because of problems of identification, the variations in film titles between different countries, different versions of the same film, questions of co-production and nationality, of when a television film counts as a film. . .

Many of the smaller countries, with the least film production to take into account, already have reasonably complete records of their national production, have indeed somewhat concentrated on national filmographies. Belgium, Holland, Denmark and Portugal apparently lead the way. Italian records, particularly for the silent years, are also quite comprehensive, though this owes more to the initiative of magazines such as *Bianco e Nero* and other unofficial sources than to efforts by the several Italian archives. Geoffrey Nowell-Smith, the director of the filmography project, has to hope that the three countries with the most titles to record and the most work to do can be brought up to scratch: France,

Britain and Germany, where the former East Germany has a much better record in cataloguing and general documentation than the West.

It would be a pity, some of the LUMIERE planners argued, to restrict this filmography to the twelve countries of the European Union. Its scope was consequently extended to bring in the other Scandinavian countries and Austria (though not Switzerland, which had registered its lack of enthusiasm for joining the Union). A thorough European filmography will be a remarkable addition to the historical record, a new tool for film scholarship. The next logical step would be to proceed to the listing of archive holdings, establishing the history not merely of what films were made, but of how many have survived, what state they are in and where they can be found. Such projects, once embarked on, have a way of developing their own momentum. But they also call for funding, not merely from the fairly modest amounts put up by the EU but from the archives themselves, or from governments which might be more ready to advance from a LUMIERE launching-pad.

The cinema's hundredth birthday gives archives throughout the world their greatest moment of opportunity. It won't come again, and must be taken. Many people doubt whether cinema, as such, has much of a future, but there can be no question that it has a past, and the custodians of that past no longer have to convince authority – still less the public – about its relevance and worth. FIAF and its members have won most of the theoretical arguments; to go further, they have to find the practical projects that can hope to attract investment. They can persuade us of the need to keep cinema's history, in other words, more easily than they can persuade us of the need to pay for it. To do that, on an international level rather than archive by archive, it may well be that FIAF has first to find more means to pay for itself.

6

KEEPERS

The only real definition of a film archive, someone said to me, is that it is a place which is able to look after its films properly. He was, of course, a preservation expert. Not all archives do look after their films properly, sometimes because they don't know how to, more often because they can't afford to. 'We keep nitrate and acetate in the same building,' a young Asian at the NFTVA's 1992 FIAF Summer School said. 'Of course we know we shouldn't be doing that, but there's no choice.' Archives with much greater resources and experience may also fall short; even in reliable Holland, a new team has had to work hard to make up for the sorry consequences of past neglect. And there are archives which may never be able to look after their films properly. The rules about storage conditions and the recommended levels of temperature and humidity can be followed in temperate countries, if the archives can afford to apply them. In tropical countries, which are also usually poor countries, the conditions for accelerating the processes of decay are all present. I asked Dr Henning Schou, Head of the NFTVA's J. Paul Getty Jnr Conservation Centre at Berkhamsted and chairman of the FIAF Preservation Commission, what, if anything, archivists in these parts of the world might be able to do to protect their films. 'Look for a cool, dry cave,' was the answer; and he was not joking.

Preservation has to be the main business of an archive, although in the language of the archivists not every film in their care is regarded as being preserved. Films in the National Film and Television Archive, for instance, could be said to go through four stages. First, there is material that is contained within the Archive but not yet fully of it; gifts, often large collections, which have to be checked, sorted, weeded for duplicates of titles the NFTVA already has from other sources, put through the formal process of acquisition. The NFTVA has taken in several major collections, from the defunct Inner London Education Authority, from firms such as Dunlop and from organisations such as the London Fire Brigade. This material is almost entirely non-fiction, on 16mm, safe enough as it is, and it has to wait its turn. James Patterson, the NFTVA's keeper of documentaries, estimated in 1992 that without allowing for any further acquisitions it would take the best part of six years to catch up with the material already in hand in his own area. Although it is a mark of the NFTVA's success that it should be seen as the automatic resting-place for such collections, the problems they present are clearly very great, the delays on the verge of becoming unacceptable, if not already beyond that.

Once a film has been given its official entry papers, as it were, it will be stored at the NFTVA's Berkhamsted centre if it is acetate and at a lonely outpost at Gaydon in Warwickshire, once an RAF bomb storage centre, if it is nitrate. Old military premises of one kind or another are favoured sites for film vaults. The Belgian archive keeps its nitrate in a fort built by Vauban; the Germans have Fort Ehrenbrechtstein; the Danes use a nineteenth-century fortress; the whole complex of the CNC archive at Bois d'Arcy is magnificently housed within the towers and walls of what was once part of the outer ring of fortifications defending Paris. Unwary visitors may find themselves trying to gain entry to a large prison block, the archive's neighbour using another part of the fortress. Gaydon itself has the bleak, windswept look of a deserted airfield, though with bunkers instead of a control tower.

Nitrate films in the archive will be regularly checked for signs of decay; acetate will only be checked at random. Clyde Jeavons, Curator of the NFTVA, claims that only some 5 per cent of the total collection is liable to be called on for programming, 'and it is always the same 5 per cent'. Other archivists would undoubtedly confirm this iceberg aspect of their holdings, with the largest archives having the largest percentage of material below the surface. Even though cinema has only a hundred years of history behind it, much of its past is already as forgotten and unvisited as that of literature and art, all the books crowding the stacks of great libraries that are never taken out and read, the paintings piled up in the basements of galleries. Until their turn for preservation comes round, the films that no one wants to see are merely kept – conserved rather than preserved.

Preservation involves altogether more positive action, copying nitrate (and so far preservation in most archives has been largely restricted to nitrate) on to acetate stock, a process which in the normal course of things results in the release of a copy for viewing. At the NFTVA, it is a complex process. In many cases, the Archive has acquired over the years a number of prints of a film, some in better technical shape than others, some more complete than others. To ensure that the material used for copying is the best available, there has first to be the stage known as technical selection – the detailed, time-consuming business of comparing these several prints. Shortage of staff produces a bottleneck; a researcher who has been promised access to a print may have to wait six months or more before it works its way through the system. The temptation would be to scamp the work, speed up the process and risk having later to duplicate a job already done; the demands of 'proper' preservation are always in conflict with the need to complete the work more quickly. Once again, the NFTVA has to cope with a mounting queue of films, a system stretched close to its limits.

Preservation is for most films the final stage: the fourth stage is reserved for the privileged few and involves restoration, a more detailed and demanding exercise. For preservation purposes, the archive checks up on its own holdings to be sure it is duplicating the best material; for restoration, it casts its net much wider, hunting down whatever may be available, from whatever source, with a view to producing something as close as possible to the definitive version of a film.

The archivists have a great attachment to nitrate. It is not merely a sentimental

Top: Bois d'Arcy, home of the Archive of the Centre National de la Cinématographie.
Courtesy of Collection Archives du film du CNC.

Bottom: The NFTVA complex at Berkhamsted.

feeling for the material on which the cinema's first masterpieces were made, or some people's sense that cinema has never been quite the same since the rich, luminous, high-contrast black and white of the 1940s. In an environment where almost all jobs are not so much open-ended as never-ending, where the un-checked collections pile up and the cataloguers can never keep pace with the new arrivals, nitrate offers the archivist one task which can actually be completed, which has to be completed, and which has even come with a deadline attached. They have always known that they were dealing with a substance which was essentially unstable, with a life span which had been estimated at not much more than fifty years, and that their priority, over all other activities, had to be to ensure that it was copied within that time; which meant, for the last nitrate films made, by the end of the century. The film would begin to go sticky and blister; it would coagulate into a gluey mess; finally, it would collapse into a brown powder. The progress was inevitable, and quite rapid once it started.

Fortunately, the cautious estimates of the life of nitrate, made by the chemists at Kodak and elsewhere, turned out in many cases to be wrong. Nitrate may survive a hundred years, perhaps quite a bit longer, in proper storage conditions, although a great deal of it will not. Poor quality stock produced during the 1940s using wood cellulose, for instance, was found to deteriorate at an alarming speed. Even the NFA, with all its checking procedures, had in the 1960s to report the total loss of several films: it had not occurred to them that such recent footage needed testing. Meanwhile, some film from the very earliest years of cinema remains as good as it ever was.

Most archivists across the world seem to accept the principle that every scrap of silent film footage deserves preservation, however slight and trivial its content, however derivative its style, however little interest it holds or will ever hold again for anyone but the specialist researcher. Only one of the many archivists I spoke to, Ib Monty of the Danish Film Museum, raised a slight scruple about the jus-tification of spending public money on salvaging such small trophies. 'We re-cently found one particular scrap of Danish silent footage,' he said. 'We were very excited. We clapped our hands. And it was terrible. Should we have spent money on it?' At Pordenone in 1992, the Dutch archive presented a whole run of films released before the First War by the French Eclair company. Eight or more fea-tured a comedian named Gontran, who in an age of great clowns must always have looked like third division material, hard-working, even over-worked, but not very funny and certainly not innovative. Even among the world's most spe-cialised and receptive audience, there was not much enthusiasm for Gontran, or for some similar one-reelers from the Eclair catalogue. Was it heresy to suggest that a smaller selection of Gontrans might have served as well for future purposes?

The Dutch argument, and a persuasive one, was the value of keeping as nearly as possible the full range of a company's output at a given time, an exercise with its own historical interest. Also, the Netherlands, a country which has not too many films of its own to preserve but has public funds available, can afford the luxury – if it is a luxury – of this kind of preservation. Where films were shot on location, there is always the historical value and charm of the unconsidered

81

background: the Los Angeles streets along which Mack Sennett's cars race and chase each other, the view of a day out in a film such as Chaplin's *Kid Auto Races at Venice*. Such glimpses over the actors' shoulders often seem more deserving of survival than anything else in the film. But the main argument for keeping every foot of every indifferent little comedy shot on a studio stage must be that it has already survived so long, when so much else has not.

There is also the notion that it is not the job of archivists to lay down standards of quality, that in their eyes all films should be equal, and that even if a film has aroused no interest for fifty years or more, there can be no guarantee that it will not be the next thing to engage a researcher's passionate attention. In some instances, such arguments might seem to have all the validity of running a hopeless animal in the Grand National in the blind faith that all the other horses might crash and fall; it could happen, but it's hardly a basis for a policy. To the archivists, however, loyal in this instance to Langlois, the only certainty is that there is no certainty. Once a film has been destroyed, it is gone for good; as long as it lives, someone, some day may find a reason to look at it.

'We are dealing with a ravaged heritage,' said Clyde Jeavons. 'I am not going to be the one to start discarding any further part of it.' There may be a time when such difficult decisions do have to be made, or there may be a time when an archive can be confident that once material has been put through the process of preservation its security is ensured for centuries rather than merely for decades. In the end, it will come down to a question of resources, and for the moment archives with active preservation policies and space to spare can argue that they have no need even to consider weeding their stocks. One of the comforts of the long-term world in which they operate is that there are always decisions which can safely be left to the next generation.

After more than forty years of acetate production, nitrate still flows into the archives, including silent films, justifying the confidence of David Meeker, the NFTVA's keeper of feature films, that if the archivist sits with a spider's patience in the middle of his web of contacts everything will in due course come his way. Collectors still keep their private caches, and if they are breaking the law on nitrate storage conditions, there seem, happily, to have been no disasters. I was told of a semi-detached house in Norwich crammed with nitrate; of a researcher who was introduced to a pile of film cans stacked close to a domestic heater; of a collector in the Netherlands hanging on to some 700,000 feet of nitrate, some of it rare, much of it already rotting, which no one was prepared to take off his hands. Ageing collectors, lumbered with equally ageing films, may be anxious to pass them on to an archive before they and their films finally deteriorate. Collectors' heirs, who might have thought there was money to be made, often find the old films merely an embarrassment. And material still comes in regularly from the laboratories and the film companies.

In 1992, the Rank Organisation delivered to the NFTVA a large collection of original negatives from the 1940s and early 1950s. Inevitably, much of it was routine stuff, cinema's equivalent of the most nondescript sitcoms and thrillers, all the areas since occupied by television. The NFTVA rule is that all preservation

John Paul Getty Jnr. and Fred Zinnemann visiting the acetate storage vaults at Berkhamsted. Photo. Julian Calder.

work should be done from the best material available; ideally, in other words, from the original negative, unless that has itself deteriorated. Some of these Rank films had already been preserved, using the best printing material to hand at the time. Now, said David Meeker, the work would in due course have to be done again. In line with the Archive's policy of trying to keep everything British, even the films that no one will want to see again are meticulously preserved. But is it really necessary that everything should be treated in exactly the same way, that only the best will do even for these dismal little relics? If archivists were not perfectionists, they would not be archivists. All films, both David Meeker and Clyde Jeavons insisted, must be regarded as equal, the cinema fodder preserved, like the Hitchcocks and Powells and Leans, to the highest standard. It was not for them to discriminate. But if not for them, then for whom, one might ask, given the scale of the task and the limits on resources. The get-out clause is 'in due course': a second preservation exercise on these films would not be necessary until their condition demanded it. The priorities, in Clyde Jeavons's words, 'could be determined by time'.

The National Film Archive, under its then new curator David Francis, embarked in 1976 on an ambitious twenty-four year programme for preserving its nitrate holdings, systematically tackling the task which Lindgren had only managed to approach in a hand-to-mouth way. New staff were engaged to carry out technical selection; the policy was to work steadily and methodically through the collection, with the work to be done by the year 2000. If they had waited much longer they could have found themselves lumbered with huge quantities of decaying film, straining beyond their limits not only the Archive's own resources but those of the few laboratories still capable of handling this kind of work. The NFA campaign was shrewdly planned, leaving the uninitiated with a clear impression that any scrap of nitrate unlucky enough to be hanging around at the turn of the century would be not long for this world, and that its end would be short and sticky. Although the Archive knew that the situation was by no means so simple, it was assumed that as the century advanced there would be a sharp increase in the rate of nitrate decomposition.

In 1976, David Francis also wrote to Jacques Ledoux, in his capacity as secretary-general of FIAF, stressing the value of a central register of archive holdings. 'The instability rate among recent nitrate acquisitions is alarming,' he wrote. Decisions about what to copy ought to be based on knowledge of what existed elsewhere. 'I know the arguments against such a proposal, but I believe they have less validity as every year passes.' It seems worth repeating that in the 1990s such a list still does not exist, that archivists remain less well informed than they probably could be about the whole question of duplicated effort, of just who is or should be preserving what, and what material they could be working from.

In France, it was not until 1990 that the CNC Archive was able to put its own systematic plan for nitrate copying into operation, working to a completion date some five years into the next century. The delay was part of that Langlois inheritance which for so long bedevilled the French archives. Now the three main ones – Bois d'Arcy, the Cinémathèque Française and the Cinémathèque de Toulouse – have cooperative policies, with all the nitrate holdings concentrated in the charge of the CNC.

Both the British and French archives secured state funding for their nitrate preservation, although in David Francis's view the British government was not greatly concerned with the value of a national heritage. What concentrated their minds was rather the Flixborough chemical plant disaster, which highlighted the danger of letting large stocks of toxic material accumulate. Both archives hold on to the nitrate originals after copies have been made, as do many of those which have the space and facilities. Some are relieved to throw the stuff away, ridding themselves of the storage problems and the fire risk. But most archivists hate having to part with nitrate. In the long run they will have no choice, but while the film is kept it can be put to use, and there is always the chance that it may survive long enough for yet another round of copying, whenever some material better and more durable than acetate arrives.

Meanwhile, there have been two changes in the situation as it was understood in 1976. Nitrate was not deteriorating as rapidly as had been expected. The speeding up of decay towards the end of the century has not happened; or not yet. I have even heard the extraordinary statement that 'nitrate is not becoming unstable *fast enough*' – in other words, with preservation policies in place it's hard to find enough justification for work which is not yet needed. The second development, which most archivists did not really wake up to until the late 1980s, was a quite unexpected hazard to preservation: the vinegar syndrome. When acetate begins to decay it gives off acetic acid, accounting for the vinegary smell when a can is opened. Acetate, everyone had assumed, had an altogether longer life span than nitrate; it was 'archival material', where nitrate was not. But the vinegar syndrome opened up the alarming possibility that all the copying had merely been from one short-lived substance to another. And the sickness can spread, like a virus, between films in storage.

In the late 1980s, Victoria Wegg-Prosser was doing research on the *This Week* television series, footage shot on film in the 1950s and now stored in the NFTVA. She found that some of the material was already badly affected by the vinegar syndrome. In this case, the magnetic soundtracks had been kept in the same cans as the films, a procedure now known to be risky. But such discoveries about material less than forty years old, beginning to fall apart while in the supposedly safe hands of even the most reputable archive, show how precarious and uncertain the whole business of film preservation can be.

The archives' concentration on nitrate preservation had been so thorough, and the efforts to raise the money to pay for it so demanding, that they had hardly had the energy or resources to consider anything else. The problems involved in keeping colour film were well understood, but to appreciate a difficulty is not to solve it; in this case, the expense was not to be contemplated. And the problems of keeping acetate had barely been seriously considered. The NFTVA, for instance, has not systematically checked its huge acetate holdings. This would be an extremely time-consuming, labour-intensive exercise, which at the end of the day might leave the Archive not a great deal wiser. Until a quick, reliable and easy system for checking acetate can be developed, comparable to the test for nitrate, a laborious exploration of the collection would weed out films already wounded but give little warning about incipient casualties. Researchers at Manchester Metropolitan University, among the experts in this field, have been developing methods of stabilisation, but at present these work only in laboratory conditions, not on the 'industrial' scale demanded by an archive operation.

The established archives have as yet no reason to be excessively concerned. Their random checking has suggested that 'vinegar' has so far affected only a small minority of films, that these are the first stirrings of yet another problem for the present generation of archivists to hand on to their successors. This is not the case in tropical countries, such as Vietnam, where the syndrome struck earlier and whole collections of films are seriously at risk. Archivists can be fairly confident that the acetate prints they have made themselves, in copying from nitrate originals, will be secure for many years. These prints will not have suffered at any stage from poor storage or handling. Some archivists, suggested Anna-Lena Wibom of the Swedish Film Institute, would really rather like to see movie prints go straight from the labs to the security of their vaults, 'without all that tiresome business of screening in between'.

The main risk must be to the prints now approaching fifty years old, the early acetate films, where the NFTVA often holds only a single copy which may have been in no very happy state even when it arrived. Might there be more *This Week* cases, I asked Anne Fleming, the NFTVA deputy curator, perhaps involving material filmed for television, less well cared for originally than cinema films? The inevitable answer: 'We just don't know.' And until some more durable material can be found, with a new polyester film base the strong candidate, the only course for an archive is to continue doing what it has always done, copying the endangered nitrate on to acetate, though now knowing that this does not really solve its problems. Clyde Jeavons spoke, with reason, of the 'tyranny of copying' from which archives can never be free. There would also be the problem, again for the future, of securing finance for full-scale preservation programmes if it were known that the whole thing would have to be done again every fifty or even every hundred years. If that were the case, the only answer would have to be a return to strict selection.

In many ways, film storage is still an area of imponderables, where new discoveries are regularly being made. Nitrate and acetate are affected both by temperature and by humidity, with water now being known to play a major part in the decomposition process. The most recent advice to archives is that they could store their films in somewhat less cold temperatures than had previously been recommended, with the advantage of keeping them drier. This inevitably leads to criticism from some archivists about 'moving the goalposts' – complaints that they can't keep up with recommendations which are constantly changing, even if they are in a position to control temperature and humidity so finely. To take all the moisture out of the atmosphere is not a viable option; it might preserve the base but would dry out and crack the emulsion. 'Film,' as Henning Schou put it, 'is a fairly complicated sandwich of ingredients.' Even the best storage conditions add up to a series of compromises, and not too many archives can afford the best conditions.

Refrigerated and relatively dry storage would greatly prolong the life of all films. In a large proportion of colour prints, the cyan (blue-green) dye is the first to fade, losing some 10 per cent in a mere seven years or so at ordinary temperatures. If the temperature is lowered by six degrees, said Schou, the effect is to double the life of the film. If it were possible to store colour film at a temperature of minus 18 degrees Celsius, it would take some 2,000 years before the dye fading could be perceived. (This, at least, is the theory.) What archive, however, could possibly meet the cost of that kind of refrigeration?

A famous, fortuitous discovery in 1978, at Dawson City in the Yukon, demonstrated the value of freezing conditions for nitrate preservation. The films involved, ordinary cinema prints from the second decade of the century, had reached the end of the distribution line when they arrived at Dawson City. Rather than ship them back, they were dumped in an old swimming pool. They were left there, frozen over, until excavations took place in 1978, and apart from a thawed top layer they proved to have survived rather well. Should the archives have been putting their money into refrigeration plants, rather than into copying the films? I have heard this suggested, though not by anyone in the archive movement.

When all the unstable material has at last been copied, it will 'take the urgency out of it', Henning Schou said. Most archives hardly began to feel that sense of urgency until 1980 or later, and some of those that had understood the situation had been starved of resources. Only the former Soviet Union and the Eastern bloc countries can equal the National Film and Television Archive's long-term preservation record. Everyone else is in the process of catching up, and aware that time is running out.

A questionnaire sent out to the archivists in EU countries in 1992 asked them, among other things, about the state of play on their nitrate programmes. The Danes had already copied all their features; Spain and Greece were among countries having less than 100,000 metres to deal with; Portugal had 500,000 metres; Belgium 2.5 million metres, Germany and Italy both 6 million, France 20 million and Britain 30.5 million. That Britain, in spite of its flying start, had by far the largest quantity of nitrate still to cope with reflected both the size of the collection, including great quantities of early newsreels, and also a change in the preservation policies which had been adopted in 1976.

One change, made in the wake of the decision to acquire all British material, was that this should be the area on which the NFA concentrated its preservation work. The primary objective, as Clyde Jeavons put it, must be 'to protect British (or British-related) films to the highest possible standard'. Films from other countries are acquired as they always have been for study and screening, but they are no longer copied. Lindgren himself had conceded in 1967 that this might be a possibility for the future, though he had insisted that none of the necessary conditions were yet in place. By the 1980s, archives had learned to trust one another, or had at least been forced to behave as though they did. Worldwide, each now concentrates on its own national production; the cost is quite high enough, without repeated duplication of effort. Michelle Aubert took very philosophically a decision by Warner Bros to remove their films from the CNC archive. 'Why should I spend my budget on saving American films?' The original idealist philosophies have yielded, as usual, to economic reality. And as the archives explore their own collections, they also make unexpected discoveries, previously unidentified films, perhaps only recorded under the title by which they were distributed in the country concerned, which can be shipped back to where they originated so that the preservation work can be done there.

The second NFA policy change was also the result of a mixture of economic factors and changing public attitudes. Archivists everywhere agree that it has become increasingly difficult – and clearly it was never easy – to persuade anyone to part with money for the purpose of preserving film for long-term needs. The old arguments about posterity, future generations and so on are not well received; the demand is that films should be available now, that archives should be seen to be earning their keep by meeting the present pressures on them. 'Preservation with a purpose,' as Wilf Stevenson, the director of the BFI, likes to describe it.

The NFTVA, consequently, no longer works its way systematically through the collection, and a target set originally at about 5 million feet to be copied each year has been dropped to less than half that. Nitrate is now copied either because it is becoming unstable and has to be dealt with (a reversion in effect to the original Lindgren approach), or because some particular film is in current demand. A large part of the preservation work is, in the jargon, access-related. Although there is the sternest insistence that the requirements of access should never be allowed to jeopardise the basic needs of preservation, some experts may conceivably wonder whether 'never' might in the future be allowed to slide into 'hardly ever'. Ironically, the more the archivists have become aware of the need to preserve, the more inexorably they have been put under pressure to make available.

There has hardly been any National Film and Television Archive budget for preserving either acetate or colour film, even though these now represent getting on for half the whole history of cinema. Any preservation work has to be financed by taking money from the nitrate budget, and accepting that the nitrate programme can reasonably now be extended by a number of years. Because of the emphasis on silent films, this archive, along with most others, also has no staff specialising in the techniques of preserving sound. 'The images were stunning,' said Henning Schou of the restored version of *Henry V*, 'but the sound left a good deal to be desired.' The concentration has been on preserving picture quality, though the soundtrack is also a major component of the film and presents its own technical problems.

By the same token, the archives have not really caught up with colour. For years colour preservation, in their terms, meant the tinting and toning of silent films, or the occasional pioneering Technicolor films from the 1930s, a *Becky Sharp* or *Wings of the Morning*. At some fundamental level, one feels that colour still tends to be thought of as something a little unusual, not as the basic stock in trade of virtually all film-makers for the last thirty or forty years. Concentration on the area of cinema seen to be most immediately at risk was inevitable; in the case of the older archives, it was where they began. But for many archivists the problems presented by silent films seem now to belong effectively to the past: they have been solved, or at least the way to solve them is clear. The issues only now beginning to be tackled, and for which hardly anyone has any money available, look more daunting, more expensive, and more difficult to confront.

When Martin Scorsese began his campaign about colour fading in 1980, he was alerting the public and his fellow film-makers to the forces gradually degrading films, but telling archivists nothing they had not already known. His cry that he had seen 'a pink leopard' (Visconti's *Leopard*) echoed round the movie world. Later, film-makers were to engage in other battles in defence of the integrity of their work. In the mid-1980s there was the war against colorisation, the tinting of black and white pictures on videotape to make them more acceptable to television audiences. (Should archives be adding colorised versions to their stock of materials for preservation? It could be argued that they should, though fortunately this need not concern the European archives: colorisation has hardly crossed the Atlantic.) In 1991, George Lucas and Steven Spielberg were among those arguing that the 'moral right' copyright safeguard for artists should be extended to American film-makers, partly as a defence against the possibility of electronic tampering with films. 'It is not going to be long in the future,' said

George Lucas, 'before an actor who has become unacceptable for whatever reasons of politics or marketability might be . . . electronically replaced by another actor . . . I see a future of indifferent copyright-owning corporations with unlimited power to tamper continually with filmed dramatic work as if they were revising an acceptance speech.' Another nightmare, perhaps, not only for film-makers but also for archivists, and another argument for ensuring preservation of the originals.

The later campaigns were largely efforts to apply moral pressure. Scorsese's publicity yielded positive if limited results. Eastman Kodak launched a new low-fade colour stock, ensuring a considerably longer life for new prints – though one still measured only in decades. But the major problem for preserving colour, both for the film companies, which should be able to afford to cope with it, and for the archives, which can't, is one of expense. The cost of copying colour is 'much higher' than for black and white and the 'difficulty factor considerably higher', said Tony Cook of the NFTVA's preservation centre. The method is to make black and white separations from the original. 'The only way to ensure that the black and white separations can in fact be reconstituted to produce a composite colour copy is to do just that – to make the copy. So you have to make the separations, then make a colour negative from them, then the colour print. Then you check the colour print quality, and put the black and white away in the vaults for preservation.'

At 1992 prices, the cost of this exercise was reckoned at an average of £30,000 for each film. Cook emphasised that film companies may not be able or willing to meet this kind of expense. 'If it is a matter of the company surviving or the films surviving, they will have to choose the company.' There is probably no film archive in the world which could contemplate such expense, except on the basis of very special efforts, probably paid for by sponsorship, to save special films. The film industry, on past evidence, can be relied on to do everything necessary to preserve films with a reasonably long-term commercial life, but be prepared to let the rest go. A company such as Disney, with an impeccable preservation record based on the policy of treating each of its major cartoon features as a permanent asset to be regularly reissued, may throw nothing away. (Though even Disney has shown no great interest in its own very early black and white cartoons.) Where a film has been made by a small independent company, however, and released by a firm which may long since have gone out of business or merged with another, the chance of the industry taking care of its own has to look slim indeed. Effectively, the preservation of colour films in large numbers, and as a matter of routine, seems to hinge on two possibilities: a concerted plan involving the archives and the world's film industries, a kind of cooperation which so far exists only on the smallest scale; or the looked for breakthrough, which will bring a dramatic reduction in costs and a promise of far greater durability.

Another archive rescue operation involves films made for the big-screen formats which are no longer in commercial use – VistaVision, Cinerama, Todd-AO and so on. The NFTVA has VistaVision prints which cannot be screened in their original form, although these are films which will also be available in standard 35mm. The 'good used' print would not be of much value in keeping Cinerama, where quality of the image was the essence of the process. The best that can be done is to endeavour to retain some examples of these processes, from a recent but rapidly abandoned phase of cinema, with the idea that at some time the technology for screening them may come back into use (as the Bradford Museum of Photography, Film and Television in 1993 revived Cinerama). There is also a case for archives keeping the special lenses and other equipment needed for such processes. How much money should be spent on such salvage operations, however, has to be another question.

Archive costs, like those of the National Health Service, have the potential to go on rising almost indefinitely, as more material involves more complex, elaborate and expensive processes. And this at a time when all the pressure has been to cut back, and archivists are inclined to remind you of what it costs them to carry out such an elementary operation as replacing rusty film cans with new ones. All film preservation seems to become a matter of juggling a range of options and compromises, and there are many areas in which it is recognised that the difficulties are not of a kind which could easily surrender to more money. If the older archives know what they should be doing, but struggle to afford it, many of the newer ones are handicapped by a shortage of expert technical knowledge and of laboratories equipped to carry out highly specialised work. There are many places around the world where it is all too likely that films are rotting on the shelves, and will continue to do so.

Money, however, solves many problems. When the National Film Library was in its infancy, a press article wistfully drew attention to MOMA's Rockefeller grant and the contrasting circumstances of the two archives. Many years later, the National Film Archive found a patron richer, more munificent and more imaginatively generous than the Rockefeller Foundation – the remarkable philanthropist John Paul Getty Jnr, himself by happy chance a film collector. 'I don't know what would have happened to the preservation programme without the Getty money,' said Anne Fleming. The Archive's conservation centre at Berkhamsted is a fine complex of buildings, settled in the Hertfordshire countryside with a kind of relaxed confidence, an establishment where means seem satisfactorily adjusted to ends.

By ironic contrast, the Museum of Modern Art Film Department had only in 1992 acquired the land to build, in Pennsylvania, its own modern preservation complex. For years it has coped with the disadvantages of storing its nitrate holdings at Fort Lee, New Jersey, not on its own premises but in the only place on America's East Coast where nitrate could legally be kept. The National Endowment for the Arts meets part of the cost of the new building programme, but the Film Department has still to depend largely on what gifts it can attract. And as Mary Lea Bandy, director of the Film Department, wryly stressed, the very rich, the traditional patrons of the great galleries and museums, are not in a mood for giving money to the arts. To prefer art to an Aids or refugee charity is to show oneself as out of touch with the world.

90

Aerial view of the NFTVA's J. Paul Getty Jnr. Conservation Centre at Berkhamsted, Hertfordshire.

Jan-Christopher Horak, who runs the Eastman House archive, made a somewhat similar point. The Reagan and Bush administrations did much to dismantle the former support mechanisms for organisations such as his own; there are now simultaneous pressures on federal, state and private funding. The Eastman House budget for film copying, he told me, had not increased since 1980, although the cost of the work had trebled. In 1992, therefore, the programme could be sustained only at a third of the 1980 level, itself not high. They were managing to keep pace with the decomposing films; they were endeavouring where possible to pass material on to other archives, since Eastman House, originally based on a private collection built up by the veteran archivist James Card, had a high proportion of European films. 'We have not lost anything that matters. Or not yet.'

These have been some of the problems for archives in the world's richest country; though one, admittedly, with little of the European tradition of public service responsibility for arts funding. And throughout the world, there cannot be many governments prepared systematically to consider the problems of preserving both film and television material, to contemplate the long-term cost or think in terms of a national plan. On nitrate, the line has largely been held, thanks in part to the fact that nitrate has so obligingly played its part, in many cases putting back its own auto-destruct mechanism well beyond the original estimates made by the Kodak chemists. It is when the vinegar syndrome begins seriously to attack films from the 1950s and 60s, and the issue of preserving colour film can no longer be treated as something exceptional, that governments may have to answer basic questions about the level of funding they are prepared or able to support. By which time, of course, what is perhaps at once the dream and the nightmare of the preservation experts may have been realised: transfer all the film to some other medium, and throw away the film.

Meanwhile, a reminder of the essential fragility and vulnerability of film came, if one were needed, with the severe fire in July 1993 at Hendersons Film Laboratories in the London suburb of Norwood. Hendersons is one of the few laboratories which still specialise in work on nitrate, and is much used by the National Film and Television Archive. Some experts dispute the assumption that nitrate can ignite spontaneously – apparently it is found to be reluctant to do so in laboratory conditions. But the fire at Hendersons, like so many of the nitrate fires on record, certainly took place in exceptionally warm weather, over the second weekend of Wimbledon, when temperatures in the region of 100° Fahrenheit were being recorded on the Centre Court.

The fire tore through two nitrate storerooms, and with the inevitable explosive, fireball effect spread beyond them to other areas which also contained safety film. Incidentally, it provided some ammunition for one of the many long-running arguments among archivists – one which I was advised 'not to waste too much time on' – as to whether plastic or metal makes the better container for reels of film. John Lucas of Hendersons told me that although in the worst hit areas the plastic in some cases melted into the film, there were also two films elsewhere virtually next to each other: the original negative of *The Belles of St Trinian's*, in

92

metal cans, and a Bowery Boys picture, in plastic. The poor *Belles* fried (though the NFTVA of course has the film in safe keeping); the Bowery Boys survived almost unscathed.

The NFTVA suffered a number of serious losses, including its restoration print of *A Matter of Life and Death*. Of 384 Archive films at Hendersons, some 40 per cent were reckoned to have been damaged or destroyed. In few cases, however, if any, would this mean the destruction of all traces of a film. Ironically, the irretrievable damage was probably worst in the area of acetate, without the back-up of preservation copies: a unique 16mm amateur film, for instance, which had been sent for copying by one of the regional film archives. In such a case, there would not even be the small consolation of insurance. The NFTVA policy, along with that of others, is to insure its copies, with a known replacement value, but not the originals.

Other material lost or damaged included a large batch of original negatives from the golden years of Ealing, there to be copied for a season at the Barbican Cinema. It seems immensely sad that the originals of such films as *Whisky Galore!* and *Passport to Pimlico* should have gone, but at the same time this was also one of those moments when an archive can feel that it has justified its existence. All the Ealing films are, of course, secure in the NFTVA, and the Barbican season was able to go ahead with copies produced from this material. It is not everywhere in the world, by any means, that could endure a loss of national production on such a scale with this degree of fortitude.

Perhaps the saddest of the many casualties were negatives of films by Satyajit Ray, which suffered when the fire attacked the area where acetate was kept. Severe damage was done to the negatives of *Pather Panchali*, *Aparajito*, *Jalsaghar* and *Devi*, and disastrous damage to *The World of Apu* (eight out of eleven reels listed as 'missing') and *Teen Kanya* (seven out of ten reels of the sound negative and three of the picture negative 'missing'). Merchant Ivory had acquired the films with a view to reissuing them in the United States, where some of Ray's films have been distributed illegally via poor-quality prints, and where there is a new, young audience to be introduced to his work. They were at Hendersons because a good deal of specialised work was called for.

Ismail Merchant showed me an expert technical report on the condition of all the Ray negatives that could be inspected, prepared before the disaster at Hendersons. It revealed the frightening vulnerability of the work of even the greatest film-makers, in countries unable to afford the back-up systems and safeguards of Western industries and archives. Of *Pather Panchali*, for instance: 'The original negative is in poor condition. Each reel has many tears in the picture area...in many reels bits of lost footage have been replaced with blank spaces. Three of the twelve reels are considerably deteriorated from the "vinegar syndrome". Several reels contain copy (dupe) negative sections replacing previously damaged scenes of original negative. . .' The negative of *Kanchenjunga*, Ray's first colour film, made in 1962, had already succumbed to the vinegar syndrome and been destroyed. When the negative of *Jalsaghar* arrived in London, Hendersons found the general condition poor. 'However, our major concern is the mould

Satyajit Ray's *Jalsaghar*. The original negative has suffered damage, first from mould eating into the emulsion, then from fire.

spores throughout the negative. The mould has eaten into the emulsion causing severe damage. There is little one can do about this . . .'

These are not films from the dark ages of cinema, but made within the last forty years, products of the East's busiest film industry. The Indian archive holds preservation material on only about half Ray's thirty-odd films, although it has fine-grain master positives on the six films sent to London. The NFTVA holds only fifteen of Ray's films, and its copies of the damaged originals had evidently been made from these same negatives and repeated their defects. Early reactions of shock were followed, happily, by greater optimism: Ismail Merchant believed that he had tracked down sources in various countries from which new copies could be made, possibly to better effect than by working from a negative already as severely injured as that of *Jalsaghar*. But this whole story illustrates the risk not only from fire but from poor storage and handling. Film preservation is a precarious business. It would be wrong to assume that in modern conditions not much ever finally goes missing.

7

SERVICE INDUSTRY

Access is the watchword, one might almost say the talisman, for the modern film archives. They talk about it all the time, practise it, worry about the ways in which they can make themselves and their services more available to the public. For years, the archives lived in a world where defence seemed the best if not the only policy. They were scared of what the film industry might do to them if they stepped out of line; apprehensive about revealing just what they had in their vaults and its occasionally dodgy provenance; nervous about any suggestion that they might seem to be exploiting their collections. Now, the mood has become almost one of exploit or die. The image of the mere passive preserver had to be discarded. The Lindgrenian archive, with the drawbridge drawn up against the outside world and the users of services tolerated rather than encouraged, would stand little chance now of survival, much less of expansion. There are many private battles within the archives about the use of resources and the emphasis on different aspects of the work, but on the surface at least everything has to be geared to the philosophy that an archive should be seen as a positive, active, outgoing sort of place. All museums, somebody said to me, have had to become part of show business; without much, as a rule, of what most museums have to show, the archives have adopted the same theory of survival.

There is some irony in the timing. Public interest in those areas of cinema which might traditionally be thought of as the archives' concern is not high. Quite possibly, it is at its lowest point since the 1930s. America has always effortlessly dominated world markets; now it rules imperially over them. It is a domination exercised not by the number of films so much as by the most con-centrated, sophisticated exploitation of the half-dozen or so pictures that can be sold all round the world at the same time. Outside the charmed circle, every-one else struggles. There are countries in which the home-grown product can hardly hope to find screen time, except on television; where films are made for festivals rather than for real audiences, which in the long run has to be a debili-tating formula. European cinema in the late 1980s and early 1990s often looked lost and demoralised, uncertain of how to cope with the American challenge and what to do.

When the Academy Cinema complex, the most distinguished of the London art houses, finally closed its doors in the mid-80s, no attempt was made, or prob-ably could have been made, to replace it. Already, the audience prepared to make the effort of reading subtitles was sliding away. The old willingness to take a chance on a film from Greece or Hungary or Japan, and the possibility in the process of discovering Angelopoulos or Jancsó or Oshima, was not greatly in evidence. In London, the National Film Theatre was losing audiences at a time when the commercial cinema was gaining them; and programmers of art house and archive-style cinemas in Europe and North America found themselves in the same leaking boat. It was easier, said the programmers, and certainly more profit-able, to put on seasons of Pedro Almodóvar than of John Ford. Articles appeared bewailing a general decline of interest in old films. Film societies were no longer at the cutting edge (if, indeed, they ever had been) but programming to catch up on last year's commercial hits. And when some critics gave the impression that for them cinema started at about the time of *The Godfather*, and that it would be unnecessary, even unhealthy, to explore any areas more remote in time, audi-ences could hardly be blamed for taking the same tack. Old certainties had gone; and old audiences with them.

And so on: a rather dismal view of the state of things, though by no means of course the whole picture. Undoubtedly, the great majority of people watching films are now sitting at home looking at a television screen: the shared experience of cinema has been replaced by the solitary one of video, with all the changes in attitude that implies. Cinemagoing was a concentrated, structured business; one had at least to be in a particular place at a particular time, which set up a relation-ship to what was on the screen. Video is diffused, unfocused, take it or leave it, and will become even more so when pushing a button admits the viewer to a vast computerised catalogue of available entertainment. The differences in the way people now think about films are profound, and by no means to the benefit of the film archives and institutes. Among other things, they have lost the authority of their exclusivity. In the early days, their power and the strongest reason for their existence was that they had the films, and access had to be on their restricted terms. Now everyone has the films, or could have them. Some video shops, said Robert Rosen of UCLA, probably hold bigger stocks than some archives.

All this does not suggest an atmosphere in which one would expect a surge of demand for archive services. There are, admittedly, more film and media courses, but they are mostly following well-worn paths rather than drawing on specialised facilities. When the archivists discuss access, it often seems to be in terms of a potential rather than an actual need. Are people queuing up to get in? Well, not exactly. Is there some area from which increased demand can be expected, and can it be pinpointed? There might be, if the archives were in a position to pro-mote and advertise their wares. One is left with the impression that in their new enthusiasms the archivists may be creating a myth, though a valuable and perhaps a necessary one. They must be seen to be serving the public, for their future income, even if they have to find ways to build up the public to be served.

Archives have since the early days been screening films, distributing them for non-theatrical or educational purposes, showing them to researchers on their own premises. The difference is not that they are actually able to do so much more, but that these are the areas they tend to emphasise. Meanwhile, public money becomes harder to come by, researchers and teachers on reduced budgets may find it difficult even to meet an archive's quite modest charges, and television can no longer afford to mount the marathon series which drew most heavily (and profitably) on archive resources. In Britain, Thames Television's *The World at War*, from the 1970s, remains about the last of the 26-part series. No one thinks that we are going to see its like again, except perhaps when the TV industry gears itself up, as it is bound to do, to cope with the challenge of the millennium.

Archives, said Paolo Cherchi Usai of Eastman House, have 'an addiction to lying', but he added that those which don't or can't provide access 'now pretend that they do, and feel guilty about it', which must be reckoned an improvement. He was talking mainly about opening up collections to researchers, something the larger archives have always done. Even then, effective access may depend on effective cataloguing, one of the most time-consuming and least visibly productive parts of the whole archive process.

The cynical view of some entrenched preservationists, those who grudge every pound which is not spent on keeping films, is that you can find yourself with an excellent catalogue of lost films – lost while you were spending the money on cataloguing instead of on preserving. The cataloguers, with equal force, argue that there is little point in having the collection unless you know precisely what is in it, where it is, the state and condition of each film. These are never to be resolved arguments. The NFTVA cataloguing department prides itself on trying to stimulate interest and deal with specific areas; a major printed catalogue would be very expensive to produce and would go rapidly out of date. 'Areas of the collection which are in constant demand' include 'the suffragette movement, political propaganda, Jews in feature films and the work of the television playwright Dennis Potter.' More there, one might think, for the amateur sociologist than for the film enthusiast.

The most basic and effective way of making films available is obviously to programme them, and for some of the newer and smaller and poorer archives, with little or no nitrate holdings to worry about, this has to be a major activity. These are the 'programming archives', and it is a moot point whether they show to preserve or preserve to show. Of the twenty-seven European archives interrogated in a 1992 questionnaire, eighteen had cinemas available to them for public screenings (31 cinemas in all, 30 of which had fewer than 500 seats). Most of them organise their programmes in a way which adds up to some sort of repertory of classics, as with the NFTVA's contribution to the National Film Theatre. Only the Belgian archive, by long tradition, screens silent films on a regular, everyday basis, although in a very small theatre.

The programming of archive theatres, however, is becoming no easier. When the archive wants to go beyond its own immediate resources, transport and other costs can become a serious problem. And Deac Rossell of the NFT pointed out a further limitation which, although not directly relevant to the archives, certainly affects their style of operation. A few prints of subtitled films used to be kept in some handy centre, such as Paris or Amsterdam, largely for the use of the film industry itself – for information, for a producer to look at while casting a picture, and so on. Now all this sort of business is done more conveniently by way of video copies. The prints consequently are no longer there; the programmers have to look further afield, at greater expense and with less chance of picking up a subtitled copy. Everywhere in this area, falling revenues are likely to encounter rising costs.

Raymond Borde, the founder and former head of the Cinémathèque de Toulouse, has probably reflected more than most people on the question of what archives are really there for. To Borde, the routine style of repertory run-through is no longer enough; there is even a kind of bored frustration in an awareness that the same films can now be seen anywhere. Time, he suggested, has overtaken that part of the archivists' function. They should now be pulling out their rarities and putting them on the screen, so trying to recapture the intellectual high ground of their research function. Anyone, he argued, can cope with the rest. Anyone can, no doubt; but of course anyone doesn't. Still, in his view, 'Archives are not distributors, art houses, film societies or film institutes...'

Borde is concerned, as are other archivists, about the vast, untouched dead stocks that they hold. Film history has been written about the survivors, as well as by them, particularly in the days before video, when historians were often writing from rather distant memory, errors were repeated from one book to another, and historians who couldn't get at the films themselves were dependent on following trails laid down by their predecessors. Borde's suggestion is that the archives should set out deliberately to survey and explore their holdings, not for the usual purpose of technical checking but in search of lost glories, which could then be brought back into circulation. To avoid too many subjective judgments, he suggests that each archive should send in a team of two on this history-rewriting reconnaissance. 'It is necessary to reactivate forgotten films by actually looking at them.' A modern archive should see itself as essentially a centre for discovery and research. It should not 'waste time on the twentieth book about Buñuel'. They will call him elitist, he suspects. But why not?

Smaller archives, such as Borde's own Toulouse, which in 1988 had 6,000 features, are better placed to explore their collections than the large ones. Such a survey is a luxury that many could not perhaps afford, though they might consider enlisting teams of critics to hack through some of the jungle of their holdings. As it is, they tend to wait for the arrival of researchers looking to explore some particular area of cinema. Clyde Jeavons pointed out the work done on silent films when the NFA invited in the researchers after the 1978 FIAF congress at Brighton. It was 'a superbly successful academic campaign'. (So successful, incidentally, that silent films, on which much of the preservation work has been done and which have been extensively researched, are reckoned to be now more accessible territory to the experts than films from the neglected years of the 1950s and 60s.)

An exercise of this sort could no doubt be repeated for other periods, but it would still be a matter of pointing researchers in a particular direction, rather than Borde's notion of a journey into the unknown. The attraction of this suggestion, of course, is precisely that no one knows the answers. Perhaps we have got film history all wrong, though one rather doubts it. Perhaps the hidden depths might turn out to be only shallows. The collection everyone would point to as the most likely to yield up treasure is that of the Cinémathèque Française, now lodged at Bois d'Arcy and at long last being systematically investigated.

It was largely through the initiative of David Meeker of the NFTVA that the films of Bernard Vorhaus, the American expatriate director who worked in Britain during the 1930s, were tracked down and made available for critical assessment. The NFTVA also unearthed most of the quota quickies made by Michael Powell in the 1930s, one or two of which their director might have preferred to remain buried. One way for an archive to draw attention to its holdings, to conduct a kind of exploration by remote control, is to talk about the films it does *not* have. When in 1992 the Archive published *Missing Believed Lost*, a round-up of the hundred British films it would most like to get its hands on, with the idea that publicity might lure some of them out of the grip of private collectors or other archives, the exercise was unexpectedly reassuring.

It would be a major coup to track down a copy of *The Mountain Eagle*, the only lost Hitchcock film, though its director himself regarded it as an entirely ridiculous piece of work. It is startling that *The New Lot*, the documentary on which *The Way Ahead* was based, should have vanished without trace. It would certainly be interesting to rediscover some more American expatriate work from the quota quickie era. But if Walter Forde's *The Ghost Train* (1931) comes almost at

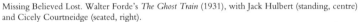

Missing Believed Lost. Walter Forde's *The Ghost Train* (1931), with Jack Hulbert (standing, centre) and Cicely Courtneidge (seated, right).

99

the top of the NFTVA list of wanted movies, it would seem that not too much in the way of British film history has so far eluded their grasp, and enough work has probably been done to ensure that there are few unexplored areas. In so far as access, in archive terminology, can sometimes seem like another word for publicity, *Missing Believed Lost* was a resounding success, the treasure hunt attracting press and public attention much more than the treasure found would ever have done.

The National Film and Television Archive itself has three small departments dealing with access matters, one concerned with the public and two with filmmakers and the industry. Not, of course, the general public: the trade would not, or at least has not, sanctioned a service on that scale; and in any case, if the NFTVA were to throw open its doors and advertise its facilities, it could not hope to cope with increased demands. The stock of viewing prints, currently some 20,000, is in the charge of the viewing service, and anyone with proper credentials engaged on a research project can apply to see them, at a small charge. Along with film students and researchers, those using the service include historians, researchers into costume, architecture, design, theatre and so on. (The viewing service also supplies prints to the National Film Theatre, regional film theatres, festivals and foreign archives.)

When a viewing print does not already exist, the preservation process can be put into operation to provide it, under the policy that the purpose of preserving

Missing Believed Lost. Arthur Woods' *Dangerous Medicine* (1939), with Elizabeth Allan.

films is to make them available. This, in turn, puts the viewing service in the hands of the technical selectors and film repairers at Berkhamsted, the areas where the bottlenecks build up. If a researcher needed passionately and urgently to see a film, could a video be made quickly, assuming that the user was prepared to meet the considerable cost? The answer from Elaine Burrows, keeper of the viewing prints, was a fairly decisive no – with the addition that 'I don't approve of private medicine'. It is stressed that the NFTVA should be used as a last resort, not as a shortcut to films which may be readily available in a distributor's catalogue or a video shop. But if the NFTVA is the researcher's last and only chance, and if the material has to be printed before it can be seen, there is bound to be a wait of months rather than weeks.

Regular researchers appreciate the problems, would probably concede that access must yield right of way to preservation. But one of the problems of researching film is that there is no browsing, as in a book library, no chance of a quick glance at a contents page, particularly when, as at the NFTVA, there is no computerised subject index for non-fiction material. And there is no doubt that people more used to orthodox libraries, perhaps expecting to complete a complex job in a matter of days, can find the delays inevitably imposed by an archive frustrating. The National Film and Television Archive has a long-standing reputation for inaccessibility to live down. Making more films available more quickly is the not always easy way forward.

It was probably to counter the NFA's old reputation that Ernest Lindgren in 1958 set up the Production Library, a direct service to film-makers and the closest that the Archive comes to a straightforward commercial operation – other than the Stills, Posters and Designs Library, which sells copies of original stills to customers. The Production Library was launched with some trepidation, the usual apprehension that it might be stepping on trade toes. In fact, somewhat to Lindgren's surprise, he was able to report in 1967 that it had proved popular with the industry, as a direct route into a collection widely regarded as impenetrable. As so often, hostility was assumed which did not actually exist.

At the outset, the Library existed largely to provide material for the makers of compilation and other films, with a small service to television. In the 1990s, with its revenue increased tenfold over a decade or so, it is almost exclusively used by the television companies, providing material for some 200 programmes a year. Its services are called on by programmes across the whole range of television, from compilations of archive footage, historical documentaries of all kinds, to commercials. The Archive adopts a position of strict neutrality on the uses to which its material is put, always assuming that the potential user has succeeded in satisfying the owner of the film rights.

As so often in archive matters, the rights holder occupies the central ground: rights must be cleared, permissions obtained, a fee negotiated. At that point, the TV programme-maker can obtain his footage from the NFTVA, with a second charge involved. It was this problem of collecting double fees for a single transaction, evidently seen by some users of the service as so unreasonable that they 'forgot' to detail the exact amount of film they were using, or to pay the Archive, which led the Production Library to charge for the footage taken rather than, as is the more usual practice, for that actually used. This system, which caused considerable ill-feeling, was abandoned in 1993 for something closer to a handling charge, except where the NFTVA itself owns the copyright. In the same way, not all television programmes which use archive material have credited the NFTVA, as though a public service did not require an acknowledgment already given the company which was the basic source of the film. And, once again, there is the problem of footage which is not already printed up, where even the making of a video copy, the style in which television prefers to receive the material, takes time.

The Production Library can react at speed. If something such as an obituary programme is involved, said Christine Kirby, who runs the service, material can be despatched from Berkhamsted to London on the day. In general, however, programme-makers certainly expect a speedier service from the newsreel companies and from the other London archive, the Imperial War Museum Film Department. Here, almost all the footage is crown copyright. The IWM can itself directly negotiate the fees, without the delay involved in clearing rights. As more and more films go out of copyright, the NFTVA may begin to approach this happy position. Already, it owns all the rights in the complete run of Topical Budget, one of the early British newsreels.

In the old days, which in television terms tends to mean the 1970s, producers would send professional researchers to look out material, people who knew their way around the archives. In the straitened 1990s, the professional researcher has become a luxury television can't always afford, and the producer's secretary or a junior member of the production team may be called into service. Several of the archivists I spoke to confirmed their experience of this sort of economy, which means that the old news film seen on television may increasingly become the more obvious rather than the recondite. The recycling of old footage for instant nostalgia has become a television industry in its own right, and as the researchers need more help, the expertise of the archivists comes increasingly into play. Occasionally, mistakes are made. One producer, needing footage of a particular Japanese submarine, despatched a researcher who approved the material on offer and put in an order for it to be printed up. The producer, however, was better informed than the researcher: the submarine was not the right one, and the bill for the footage was not met. The NFTVA, as usually happens, got its money in the end. But such are the hazards of supplying factual material, which may from the outset have been identified wrongly, or not at all, in spite of all the cataloguers' efforts.

The problems of sustaining such a service are experienced not only at the sharp end, in dealing with the buyers of material; there is also pressure on the support staff needed to prepare and transport it, an area in which greater demands for access rarely produce staff increases. It's a sign of the problems that although the NFTVA has a Telecine machine, used for transfer between film and tape, it was for years unable to employ it to speed up operations because the salary on offer was not enough to attract an operator. A minor problem compared with that of the foreign archivist who told me of a theatre left idle because no one could pay the projectionist.

Christine Kirby argued that the industry does rather well out of the Archive, not least in terms of free storage for films which are secure in its hands and might otherwise be left to take their chance in laboratories. The third of the NFTVA's access departments, and significantly the one experiencing the most rapid growth, is Donor Access, in effect a service for maintaining good relations with people and companies that have deposited films and with what are rather quaintly referred to as 'authorised third parties' – anyone with a legitimate interest in a film, from companies which have taken over the rights, to actors and their families who might want a video copy. By English law, at least, purchase of the rights in a film does not entitle the new owner to make a claim on prints of it in an archive, although some have tried to scare archives into handing them over and some archives have yielded to pressure. But the old notion that once a film entered the Archive the prison doors had effectively closed on it no longer applies – if, in practice, it ever really did. There has to be a busy traffic with rights owners wanting to get at their material, to have it copied, even on occasion to remove it.

Archives have to take a philosophical view of such dealings: part of their improved relations with the trade depends on their readiness to allow themselves to be used in this way. Most agreements with donors at least ensure that the NFTVA has the right to make a copy of any film leaving its premises, either temporarily or for good, although with colour films of course this could hardly be a viable option. Jane Hockings, who is in charge of the service, reported ' no insurmountable problems', although as with everyone working in this area her job appears to be a matter of juggling demands and priorities. The original donors of the films, it seems, are more likely than their successors to sympathise with an archival point of view. And access by way of video has certainly made matters easier, while at the same time increasing the expectations of speed from people used to a faster-moving video technology.

Video is in effect the only route by which an archive could make its collection, or large areas of it, more or less instantly accessible, the dream of a push-button future, of researchers sitting in front of their screens, able to call up material to order. The problem, apart from the usual one of cost, is that the video is not the film, but a substitute for it. Also, video technology has been far more volatile than that of cinema. Apart from the flurry of new formats in the 1950s, when the cinema was throwing everything into its battle with television for audiences, screen systems have remained remarkably stable over the years. Any cinema, anywhere, has always been able to screen a 35mm print. One reason for this stability, of course, has been the reluctance of everyone involved to contemplate the re-equipping of cinemas all around the world with every introduction of a new format.

With video, no such considerations apply. Technological change has provided advantages to the professionals, in the form of tape that is easier to handle and on which more information can be stored. And an equipment industry dealing with the home market can happily and profitably introduce changes at regular inter-vals – from black and white to colour, from one tape format to another, from the standard receiver to the satellite dish. One reason that high-definition, large-screen television has developed so much more slowly than was originally predicted may well be that the domestic market is not yet ready for it: this is an area in which market forces call the tune. Archives, providently, have held back from moving too rapidly. Any archive which had gone for quick access by putting large parts of its collection on to two-inch tape, for instance, would have found itself lumbered with stocks of obsolete tapes and only a few ageing machines on which to play them.

Archivists, in any case, feel strongly about video, a subject for contentious and repeated discussion at their congresses. Some, such as UCLA, take a relaxed view: this is the inescapable technology, to be lived with, exploited and used to the general benefit. Some are neutral, happy to show researchers the film itself, but also quite pleased if they choose video because it saves wear and tear on the print. And there are those for whom video is seen not just as the thin edge of the wedge but the wedge itself, driven into the environment where film should remain sacrosanct. A television set, said the veteran Austrian archivist Peter Kubelka, is no more than 'a piece of furniture with a picture on it'. Video was fit for nothing more than 'stupid studies', not for the proper business of research. He added a caution: 'Once you make video-tapes, rather than preserving film correctly, the pressure is off and you are left for ever with your tapes.' Gabrielle Claes, of the Royal Belgian Film Archive, argued that even film school students now watch films on video as a matter of course: there must be one surviving bastion of the old, authentic values, one place at least where they can be reminded what film really is. Disarmingly, she added that she could afford to take such a stand because the demands on her service were not excessive. Eileen Bowser of the MOMA Film Department took the same firm line: video is not film, should not be regarded as identical, and archives should not take the easy option with it. On their premises, researchers would see film as it should be shown.

Of course, they are right. Without going into arguments about the difference in principle, and so in perception, between the illusion of the persistence of vision provided by 24 frames per second and television's constant process of scanning, there is no question that the video image falls short of the contrast effects of a good 35mm print, simply records less in the way of visual information. Video makes a very efficient tool for studying content; when it comes to style and effect, the film itself has to be the thing. And, some might even say, the film in its correct context, screened in a cinema with an audience.

The movie was not conceived as some laboratory object for solitary study, or for showing in the kind of cinema actually championed by Peter Kubelka, an all-black setting, with minimum distraction from the environment, where spectators would be partitioned off from their neighbours. Many directors, Alfred Hitchcock most notably, have constructed their films partly on the basis of what an audience will be doing and thinking, how it can be lured into com-placency and jolted out of it. However often one may have seen *Psycho*, it still works in a cinema because of the tension building up in the audience; seen on television, the film looks almost like a blueprint of itself. A casualty of film research conducted in laboratory conditions tends to be the dangerous side, the power of performance, the awareness of risks negotiated with an audience. 'Films are seen on video; in a cinema they are experienced,' said David Puttnam, who also feels that video makes it much too easy for directors to crib from the classics, to run through particular sequences and note just how they were constructed for effect, without too much attention to the context. All of which adds to the trend towards a cinema of tricks rather than substance.

The archivists who try, at least in their own strongholds, to resist the inevitable advance of video must know, however, that they are fighting not merely the future but present preferences. They are attempting to save from themselves film students who actually choose video, for its familiarity, its ease of transport and handling, who prefer fast forward to reel time. Film school students may not have grown up as regular filmgoers: cinemas remain for some of them unfamiliar places, and a film is thought of as video on a big screen.

In other areas, some but not all archivists are equally adamant that standards must be maintained. Should they, for instance, be prepared to send out stretched prints of silent films, so that the pictures stand a chance of reaching a wider audience in cinemas not equipped to show them at the proper speed? 'You must adapt the machines to the films, never the films to the machines,' would be the purist argument. Should dubbed films be regarded as acceptable, particularly in countries such as Italy, where dubbing has always been standard film industry practice? Even the anti-video argument may fall down when someone from the Middle East argues that in his country video is effectively the only way many films can be seen at all. Archives should try to hold out for proper projection standards and respect for original screen formats, it is generally agreed. They should not send out 'bad objects'. But the NFTVA Production Library, for instance, allows its clients to make panned and scanned copies or tapes of Scope films, if that is what they want, even though the Archive's own preference might be for letter-boxing. Even the larger archives find it hard at all points to defend perfectionist standards. Smaller archives, in this as in other areas, have to do the best they can.

There is also the question of whether, and how much, archives ought to charge for opening up their collections to researchers. Some have a tradition of free access: the Library of Congress, for instance. Some, such as the Imperial War Museum, offer a certain amount of free viewing, followed by a modest charge; many of their users, in the tradition of the Museum, will be former servicemen or their families, wanting to see some particular military action. They have copies of most of the material likely to be called on for viewing – and still on film rather than video. The National Film and Television Archive charges researchers about £7 an hour. The more expensive archives to visit, I was assured, were generally reckoned to be Stockholm, Amsterdam and the Cinémathèque Française. But there are few people who still argue in principle against charges: it has to be accepted that the viewing of film is an expensive business, that a film must be prepared, rewound and probably transported, and that someone must pay. Nor is it the archives' job, as often seemed to be assumed in the past, to subsidise education.

People outside the archive movement generally accept video more readily, seeing it as the way in which archives have to move forward if they are to get more use and value out of their collections. Time, resources and a great deal of public money have gone into preserving films: trying to extract some profit from them ought to be the next stage. Murray Weston, of the British Universities Film and Video Council, argued that entrenched habits of thinking, the emphasis for so many years on shutting up rather than opening out, may blinker archivists' views of what might be done. The NFTVA, he pointed out, has a large stock of science films, much of it unseen, unknown and forgotten. Some are now out of copyright; in other cases rights could be negotiated with people who would be glad to see even the smallest return on material long since written off. The films and the means are there, in his view, for a series of video compilations, a screen history of twentieth-century science.

Archives in Britain have been working their way towards similar ideas. It is not only a question of the modest profit that might be made from the sale of videos (and it could be modest indeed), but of public attitudes. A collection which is largely unused increasingly runs the risk of seeming merely useless. Archives must find the way to unlock more of what they have in their vaults, or seem still to be conserving material for the hypothetical needs of future generations, always waiting for demands which may never be made. Although all libraries have to contend with such questions, not all libraries have material as expensive to store and maintain as film. 'Archives *must* exploit their collections,' said Clyde Jeavons. Which means, in effect, by way of computerisation and video.

The Imperial War Museum Film Department has produced several videos, including that old standby *The Battle of the Somme*. The NFA launched a kind of pilot scheme, when a compilation video was brought out to accompany Luke McKernan's enterprising book on the life and times of the Topical Budget newsreel. The difficulty of such exercises for large archives is that sales of one-off ventures are likely to be discouraging, while a full-scale programme involves investment in both production and marketing – another distraction, as it were, from basic purposes, another example of the tension between the imperative demands of preservation and the more speculative ambitions of access. If archives are to divert money into video production they have to be sure of getting it back; and with what they have to sell, that is by no means certain.

The archives have not been slothful in working towards these new activities. Until recently, any suggestion that an archive intended to profit from its collection would have rung all the alarm bells. Not much could effectively be done until films began to creep slowly out of copyright. In America, where the legal position is more clear-cut, many films are now in the public domain. In Britain, problems still date from the inability of the 1911 Copyright Act to cope with precisely how a film should be defined: it was still seen as in the nature of a collection of photographs. Later Acts which have clarified the position have not operated retrospectively; early film copyright remains a tangled area, with rights often extending beyond the film itself to, for instance, the author of the play or novel it was based on. The most recent of the NFTVA's many bids for Statutory Deposit contains a proposal that the Archive should be given a kind of guardianship, including the right of exploitation, in cases where copyright ownership is obscure or, as often happens, untraceable. Anyone who wants to make use of a film has to make all reasonable efforts to track down the rights owner, quite often without success. There are many such cases already, and will soon be many more, and it is in everyone's interests that the films should not be indefinitely locked away because of excessive caution.

'From the moment that you begin trying to recycle the visual image,' said Victoria Wegg-Prosser, 'you will find that you owe money to somebody.' This concept of images as property remains basic, in continual conflict with the arguments about intellectual freedom, the new insistence on access as a right in itself. Traditionally, the archives have campaigned on behalf of educational and other users of material. Now that they are in the position of becoming rights holders themselves, and under heavy pressure to earn money, to look at their collections in terms of actual rather than potential value, we might see some change in their attitudes. It will be an intriguing development for archive watchers.

For the moment, however, the key to the emphasis on access has probably been the new confidence created by the 1980 UNESCO recommendation and an altogether more relaxed and sophisticated relationship with the rights owners. The commercial film industry began really to appreciate the archives from the point when a studio's own film library became a positive asset, a resource to be exploited and traded, rather than a largely unwanted collection of old movies. In some cases, it was the archives that held the only surviving prints of films, discarded by the studios in more reckless days. Many of the major companies, including most of those in Hollywood, maintain their own active preservation policies; when they pull films out of the archives, it may well be because they intend to look after them themselves. And many of the American majors have built up special relationships with particular archives: Eastman House with MGM, for instance, or UCLA with Universal. MOMA has a corner in Clint Eastwood and James Bond films, among others. Archivists, said Mary Lea Bandy, should think in terms of a responsibility to living film-makers, not only to the past. Such close links depend on trust and confidence all round, and on the film companies' assurance that in these areas at least, the collections are *not* about to be exploited.

Much of this change has come about since the spread of video, which blew a hole right through the old jealous guardianship of the prints. The pirates were still to be fought, but they had finally to be seen as a different species from the archivists and the collectors. For the archivists, too, video has to impose major changes of attitude. Film can be treated as a museum object, something of unique value. Video is casual, undisciplined, hard to pin down, even to identify; tapes can be tampered with, wiped, recycled, copies can be run off at random. Video is not a medium to be trusted, or to which the same strict standards can be applied. Film has to be preserved in the original format and the best possible printing material must be used. With video, there is no need for this: within limits, copying does not mean any surrender of quality. It is a tool, a short-cut to access, a way to bypass time-consuming procedures and so to relax pressures. Archivists who dislike video probably also dislike its free and easy ways, its rejection of the tight controls that they, as well as the rights owners, have always been able to impose. Many of them still have to come to terms with this, if they are effectively to use their collections.

At some future time, archives should be able to beam films by satellite to centres around the country. There are people who think that the NFTVA could be doing this already, as a way of opening up the use of the collection for educational purposes, extending research facilities to a wider public. Certainly, support for education has become another of the fashionable access causes. Twenty years ago, said Mary Lea Bandy, the Museum of Modern Art Film Department would have stressed its concern for the artist and the individual; in the 1990s the emphasis is rather on involvement with the community through education – not so much a change of role as of presentation and style.

In the United States and in France, particularly, cooperation with university film departments and with film schools is regarded as essential: archives should no longer wait passively for demands to be made on their services, but should engage themselves in the process, not least in educating the educators. The film schools, it is said, complain that the films are not available; the archives complain that the schools can't be trusted to look after them. But the main role for the archives is seen as that of reminding technically minded schools of film's historical tradition, persuading the instructors that exposure to movie culture, as well as its techniques, is desirable, even necessary. Archives are resolute in their view of themselves as strongholds of forgotten values.

For the larger archives which engage in these activities, the ticking clock in the background is still signalling the need to complete their nitrate preservation programmes: for all the talk about access, and the juggling of resources to achieve it, they can't escape that awareness of the original imperative. It is refreshing to visit the kind of small establishment where access really is a way of life – by necessity, certainly, but also perhaps by choice. Many countries have regional archives of one kind or another, some of them long established. In France, said Michelle Aubert, the French instinct for hoarding has led some to accumulate their own small stocks of feature films. In Britain, long before the days of the archives, it would appear that some town councils kept odds and ends of film about local activities in their cupboards.

There are four English regional archives, based in Manchester (North-West), Gateshead (Northern), Norwich (East Anglian) and Winchester (Wessex). There is a Scottish archive in Glasgow, and a Welsh film and television archive in Cardiff. All are fairly recent creations, the earliest dating from the late 1970s, and they operate in somewhat different ways, with different styles of funding and local attachments. Their archiving standards are those recommended by the NFTVA, but their allegiances are also to the communities whose histories they try to preserve.

The East Anglian Film Archive was set up in 1979, and functions on a modest grant from the Eastern Arts Association, office space and maintenance costs provided by the University of East Anglia at Norwich, and whatever it can generate in the way of income from its own remarkable range of activities. It's tiny, compact, with a staff of four, and runs on the kind of twenty-four hours a day energy that in larger concerns inevitably finds itself muffled by bureaucracy and bigness.

David Cleveland, who is head of the archive, said that he would like to think of it surviving for 'hundreds of years' as an essential record of East Anglian life. Meanwhile, its none too generous acceptance by the University and requirement to earn most of its own income leaves it precariously balanced between ambitions for permanence and the day-to-day effort of running to stand still. Its collection is made up of local newsreels, educational and sponsored films, publicity material from firms in the district, amateur records. Any nitrate it uncovers goes to the NFTVA. Occasional rarities have included, for instance, a film made by Anthony Asquith about Papworth Hospital (now known as a centre for transplant surgery) in the days when it treated tuberculosis. Films reach the archive from all sorts of sources, including private collectors. They have had to break down a notion that an archive would only be interested in old things, and persuade people to bring video into the collection.

To add to the local historical record, they are prepared to go out and make films themselves in what passes for their spare time – one about a small circus; something more ambitious about a motorway construction project near Norwich and the changes it brings to the landscape, with a contribution of £4,500 from the motorway contractors to pay for the film stock. This is on 16mm film, not video, partly because of doubts about the durability of tape, partly so that the film can be shown locally, in cinemas and elsewhere. The archive supports more than 200 shows a year, mostly presented by amateur enthusiasts for local history who select their programmes from its stock and stage them in clubs, schools and the like, incidentally recruiting more supporters for the cause.

Everything, in such a setting, depends on a network of contacts: knowing the collectors, the people with the interest to arrange programmes, the local firms which might be persuaded to chip in with a little sponsorship, the amateur film-makers who have recorded the history of a family or a town. It also depends on a community with a fairly strong sense of local identity and concern about its own history – predictably, said David Cleveland, Essex trailed behind its neighbours, Cambridgeshire, Suffolk and Norfolk. A fair part of the archive's income comes from the videos it compiles from its collection and sells in bookshops, museum shops and elsewhere: films about the Norfolk Broads, or windmills, or the American forces and their wartime air bases throughout this empty countryside. Researchers from television companies turn up to look for material, though they too report a decline from the days when someone from Thames Television would settle in for the day. And such users of services as children with school projects are admitted free. 'How could we charge them? They might go away and never come back.'

Along with all this evidence of how access works at the grass-roots level, the East Anglian Film Archive, with the University Film Department, runs an MA course for film archivists, an enterprise originally suggested to it by David Francis. This is not the only archive training course in the world, but it's still a considerable rarity and its students have included trainees from overseas archives. Close links are maintained with the NFTVA, so that students have the chance to explore the workings of a large archive as well as a small one, and the tie to the University Film Department, itself one of the best in the country, takes care of the academic qualifications.

It's a paradox that only a small organisation with a healthy concern for its own survival could cover so much ground. A major archive would think twice, for instance, before adding to the screen record by making its own films. It would probably decide that it wasn't necessary, though there could be a case for it nationally as well as locally, or would have to bring a whole department into existence for the purpose. Nor could it count on the local interest that can sustain the sale of compilation videos without too much professional marketing effort. One of the most agreeable evidences of East Anglia's sparky enterprise is its subject index, a somewhat quirky catalogue evidently compiled by human hand and so far without intervention by computer.

Farming in Autumn (1934), from a series for the classroom by Mary Field. Courtesy of East Anglian Film Archive.

On the day I visited them, they were rather pleased that they had been able to meet a request from a BBC programme which was looking for any films about sandwiches. The subject index had duly turned up a publicity film from before the war, advertising Colman's mustard as the ingredient no sandwich could do without. I tried the sandwich test on the National Film and Television Archive cataloguers, but they were only able to help if the word featured prominently in the film's title – and you would get *The Sandwich and Hythe Light Railway* thrown in as well. Such are the byways of access to the archives.

8

'OF THE SCHOLARS,
NOTHING IS TO BE EXPECTED...'

When in 1898 Boleslaw Matuszewski put forward his proposal that films should be kept for the future, he was essentially thinking of the historical record. He would no doubt have approved of the local archives, with their commitment to a region and its changing aspects. He would probably have thought well of the use of video surveillance, since one of his more startling suggestions concerned the potential value of the film record for the police. He might have been perplexed, however, that historians in general have shown so little interest in the whole conception of visual history as source material. Archives which keep it, such as the National Film and Television Archive, now have a hundred years on their shelves, and not too many people seem to be interested in using it.

Sir Arthur Elton came close to echoing Matuszewski's original title when in 1955 he wrote 'The Film as Source Material for History', one of the most significant, and certainly one of the most lucidly and elegantly argued, of the many attempts to persuade historians that film should be taken seriously. Of course, one major disadvantage of the film record (as opposed to some extent to the television record) is that it kept so close to the surface of things, history as made in public. The cameras stayed on the pavement outside Number 10 – now, of course, it is the Prime Ministers who skip on to the pavement to join the cameramen. Cinema newsreels earned, though by no means entirely deserved, their reputation for triviality. As Elton put it:

> Of scenes of one-legged men pushing turnips with their noses from Paris to Rome there is much; of boat races, crowned heads, bathing belles, railway smashes, the glossier phases of war, fashion parades, fires, murders and dance marathons, more; but of industry, technology, sociology, art, poetry, agriculture, only accidental glimpses. There are miles of men biting dogs, but much less of the stuff of history – dogs biting men.

The much-mocked cinema newsreels were never in competition with the press – except when they could briefly beat it, in excitement if not in speed of delivery, with such items as the annual Grand National treat. They were allowed their small place in an entertainment industry; and their job was to entertain. They slipped in between the two halves of a double bill, going down as easily as the ice-cream interval, meeting the demands of cinema proprietors whose attitude to their customers was almost boundlessly pusillanimous. Audiences were thought likely to be easily depressed, bored by politics, upset by anything that by any stretch of imagination could be seen as controversial. Newsreel stories were snipped, filleted, self-censored, supplied with bracing and bouncy commentaries to fit the space the exhibitors assigned to them. But press reports, after all, are not immune from manipulation.

The newsreels earned their reputation; and yet were much better than it suggests. The people who made them took them more seriously than the people who showed them; the cameramen got everywhere, and managed to film most of what mattered; an edge could be put on a commentary. If they were short on the inner workings of politics, they were long on social history, the often unconscious, unaware evidence of the way people spoke and conducted themselves, the clothes they wore and the cars they drove, all the habits and gestures that change imperceptibly over the years and which can most effectively be studied not by reading the record but by looking at it and listening to it. And if all else fails, the newsreels can always be looked at as evidence of the attitudes of the time: the way things were, and the way they were seen to be.

If newsreels had been more valued, however, historians and academics might have been persuaded that visual history should not be disregarded. 'The principal thing frustrating the proper application of film to history,' wrote Elton, 'is lack of awareness of the possibilities, and the lingering feeling, a hangover from the naphtha flare days, that it is undignified for scholars to take seriously what they often choose to call the "flicks", something associated so uncomfortably closely with the unscholarly masses. It is perhaps for this reason that most British universities have neglected the use of the film from any point of view almost to the point of perversity.'

There have, of course, been many changes and developments in the academic approach to film since 1955, but almost forty years later the neglect is still very evident, and the reasons for it are still discussed in precisely the same terms. Film is thought of as too young, said Murray Weston, to have been properly assimilated into the system, though it's now a century-old infant. Film, said Jerome Kuehl, is something for the historian's Saturday-night entertainment. To suggest that it might also be something worth taking seriously would be like recommending scholarly study of the press by way of the *Sun* and *Hello!* rather than *The Times* and the *Economist*. Does a historian preparing the biography of some twentieth-century figure at least think to call in at the National Film and Television Archive to inquire about what they might have, to see what his subject looked and sounded like? Certainly not. Or so everyone I spoke to assured me. Murray Weston could remember only one occasion on which a historian had actually quoted film references along with the more orthodox ones in a bibliography: Alan Bullock in his study of Hitler.

There are other and more practical deterrents. It is more expensive to study films than to read books, takes more time and is more difficult. Unless the researchers know their way quite well about the archives, they are up against the

113

problem that they often can't estimate the usefulness of the film without looking at it – by which time there will probably be a bill to be paid. Researchers working on subjects where film is not seen as directly relevant will seldom have grants or budgets to meet such expenses. If academic researchers were not already thinking of film as something too frivolous to bother with – or, more probably, were not thinking of it at all – the actual effort to work with it might persuade them that it is both a luxury and a nuisance. People I spoke to, both inside and outside archive circles, agreed that huge resources were still being neglected 'almost to the point of perversity'. And eventually, if the archives are to justify their work in this area, such attitudes must change, though it has taken so much longer than Matuszewski, or even Elton, thought to break down historians' allegiance to the written word as the one reliable source.

Elton made two particularly interesting points in his article. He believed passionately in the value of out-takes, all the bits and pieces of footage retained by the newsreel and other libraries, the raw material behind the tidy little edited stories that reached the screen. He wanted the National Film Archive 'boldly to enter a field it cannot ignore for much longer' and to take as much of this footage as it could lay its hands on, particularly when it came to the Central Office of Information films. It was Emile de Antonio who was to say that 'the history of the 1960s was written in the out-takes' – and to demonstrate it with his own films. And in 1992 a group of French film historians was suggesting that out-takes should be the 'new thing' for the archives to pursue.

At the same time, Elton believed in policies of strict selection, though without making it clear on just what principles choices should be made. 'The film archive library should have a declared aim on no account to receive more than a selected minimum. Otherwise, the film archivist will find himself receiving not only the baby but the bath water, the bath, the boiler, the coke bin and the coke.' His point was the difficulty of cataloguing and classifying the footage to bring it into use. His caution has not been heeded, and in this area particularly the risk is that the amassing of film becomes an end in itself because it can *all* seem relevant, that it is hard to strike a reasonable balance between over-strict selection policies and the urge to grab everything in sight. 'We become increasingly less selective, which also means less arrogant,' James Patterson said. 'As an archivist, I am not allowed to decide where aesthetic questions end and social history begins,' said Paolo Cherchi Usai in a slightly different context. Their determined neutrality is the route to taking in the coke bin and the coke.

There is one remarkable assertion in Elton's article. 'For the eight years from 1939, Britain may be the country most completely documented by film in the world.' In the mid-50s, the film libraries were awash with all kinds of official and unofficial footage, much of it dating from the war, and much of it eventually finding its way into the collections of the NFA or the Imperial War Museum. The Grigg Committee on Public Records, which issued its report in 1954, had been informed that eighteen government departments held between them a staggering 40 million feet of master material, considerably more than the entire holdings of the National Film Archive at the time. Often the departments 'had difficulty in calculating the quantity of film held by them', were not sure whether it was sound or silent, or what subjects it might concern. When Elton reported such statistics, along with estimates of the film material held by other sources, it was somehow characteristic that Ernest Lindgren should have reacted with a mild rebuke. Elton had used the word 'archive' to describe what in Lindgren's view were 'repositories of working material to be used in day-to-day production'. Exclusivity was to be maintained; though the answer had to be that today's working library could well be tomorrow's archive.

The British archive which keeps out-takes and the like as a matter of course is the Imperial War Museum Film Department. It currently holds some 70 million feet of film – or roughly 50 million feet when duplicate copies are discounted. Much of this material is the archivist's or compilation film-maker's dream: unedited footage, the raw material preserved exactly as it left the camera. In many cases, the cameraman's original notes have survived with the film. 'A researcher can actually read what the cameraman thought he was doing, as well as seeing the footage,' said the Keeper of the Film Department, Roger Smither. The time and place of shooting are on record.

The Museum is the repository for the material shot in both world wars by official sources, the authorised newsreels and other film-makers of the First War, the Army and RAF units of the Second – the Navy, at least until after D Day, chose to do without a film unit. It can also hold material on any wars involving Commonwealth forces, which brings in Vietnam via the Australian connection. Film is still shot for the services, and still finds its way to the IWM, but most of it is made for training and recruiting purposes. For later conflicts the IWM must largely depend on standard news sources, such as ITN's record of the Falklands War. It's also thin on the ground when it comes to material from between the wars. During the lull before the action in the early days of the Gulf War, 'literally dozens' of television researchers, said Roger Smither, approached the Museum for any footage on the RAF bombing of Kurdistan during the 1920s; they had, however, to go away empty-handed. And the Gulf War itself was a video war, recorded in such graphic detail but it would seem without a foot of old-fashioned film being professionally shot.

It was during the 1970s, when Clive Coultass was Keeper of the Department of Film, that the IWM was able significantly to expand its role. It follows the museum habit of making its collection available, and it is certainly used. Its earnings from material supplied to television stand at about £200,000 a year, which comes reasonably close to balancing the £250,000 bill for the Museum's current nitrate copying programme. One reason that the IWM has the reputation for accessibility which the NFTVA is still trying to establish may be that people see museums as open places, archives as closed; another is that it has evident appeal to the professional and military historians, who may have a clearer view of just what they are looking for in its particular context. But has any of these professional historians ever admitted to actually *learning* anything from looking at a film, rather than merely having existing knowledge confirmed? It would seem not.

King Edward VII filmed by an unknown news cameraman at Sandringham in 1909.
The shot was included in a compilation film, *Twenty Years Ago*.

The FIAF member archives vary in their approach to historical record film. Some keep it; some don't. Many were founded by enthusiasts for the art of the film, and remain true to that original allegiance. In the United States, the main repository for news film is the National Archives, although UCLA, for instance, has the major collection of the Hearst newsreels, and there are many other stocks of news film in archives and in more specialised libraries. In Britain, the National Film Library was from the outset left in no doubt about its own dual role. Film was to be preserved and studied 'as a record of contemporary life and manners', a purpose probably taken more seriously by many people at the time than the altogether more speculative business of keeping feature films.

The Archive's non-fiction holdings not only considerably outweigh the fiction, but they are growing at a much faster – it might seem almost uncontrollable – rate, with the addition of all the large collections from organisations which have either given up film-making or no longer want the problems and expense of storing their films. Another regular source is the laboratories, lumbered with large stocks of 16mm footage, much of it with no easily traceable owner. It's remarkable how casually the proprietors of footage often treat it, leaving it lying about in store to be disposed of years later by laboratories which, fortunately, may have no taste for junking film if it can be rescued.

The NFA took charge of the great Visnews newsreel collection, nitrate film

116

which was in danger of decay if not already getting beyond the danger point. This was essentially a rescue operation. It also holds progressively the Movietone newsreels, with an arrangement that the Archive will be responsible for copying the material and the film company will cover the cost of the stock. And it has the Topical Budget newsreels, acquired with copyright in the whole run of the company's product when the laboratories which had controlled the material went out of business. The newsreel collections are great and valuable assets, but companies with shareholders to satisfy have often been unwilling or unable to shoulder the costs of long-term preservation. The expense, from their point of view, outweighs the benefits: they are prepared to use, and eventually to discard. Willy-nilly, the Archive has had to take over the job, adding greatly to its own preservation responsibilities. The newsreel companies, however, still draw the income from the use of their footage.

When it comes to new material, it will usually not be film at all: virtually all non-theatrical, non-fiction material is now video, and its acquisition presents another set of problems. Video is undisciplined, often goes unrecorded, is hard to trace and track down. James Patterson uses the British National Film and Video Catalogue as his main source of information, but not even its assiduous researchers can locate too much of the tape that exists beyond the range of company catalogues. Video means, or can mean, more or less anything: campaigns for street crossings, or against the building of motorways, records of little local battles with authority, of election campaigns, sports events, public meetings, promotion for firms and shops. . . Much of this, if it is thought worth keeping, can more easily be corralled by the regional archives.

Voraciously, however, the NFTVA samples, selects, tries to keep up with what it can. There is no end to this material, and no obvious limitation on what might be considered 'relevant', if the purpose, as proclaimed, is to preserve the historical record 'at the densest possible level'. Traditionally, too, non-fiction film has always been much less thoroughly and reliably documented than fiction. Fewer copies of documentaries were put into circulation, the films did not on the whole get the same widespread international distribution, often they escaped the attention of reviewers. There is a lengthy paper trail to follow in the case of most features, all the way from the production records to the press reviews. Not too much of this has ever existed for documentary, and for video the records can be skimpy to the point of non-existence.

Lines have to be drawn somewhere, and at some future date one feels that they may have to be drawn altogether more stringently. The NFTVA takes the view that as long as it has the space available it can take in material, knowing that the really hard decisions as to what to do with it may not have to be made for the best part of another fifty years. The problems that seem more compelling concern ways of bringing all this footage into use. When I spoke to James Patterson, he had just been looking at some video, part of a campaign advising greengrocers on how to display their wares. The Archive was not taking it in; but if it had decided otherwise, it would have been a classic case: footage without a title, with no credits to record, anonymous, unknown, in effect having no official identity for preservation purposes other than through the NFTVA's own catalogue. Those cataloguers who grandly insist that 'a film doesn't exist until it has been catalogued' do sometimes have a point.

Many of the older archives, both in North America and Europe, have discovered considerable enthusiasm for amateur films, home movies in all their manifestations. Archivists are prepared to sit through the footage of babies on beaches, nervously posed wedding groups, jokey dashings about suburban gardens, for the nuggets of authentic social history which might otherwise go unrecorded, the story of life through the years of a family or a town, or the films shot by enthusiasts in, for instance, the colonial civil service, recording ways of life in areas where the professionals never ventured. It seems also to be felt that amateur footage is somehow purer, more authentic, less subject to manipulation for commercial or political ends. Harry Price, in the late 1930s, in his capacity as NFL Committee Chairman, had already suggested, much to the gratification and surprise of the amateurs, that they might be enlisted to record local customs and celebrations. After many years in which the archives may have felt they had their hands full in dealing with the professionals, they are again actively looking out for the amateurs, and turning up material which may be unique.

James Patterson reckoned that as much as 20 per cent of his time is spent in following up sources of amateur footage, much of it unearthed by way of television, viewing it and negotiating with its owners. The Imperial War Museum follows the same policy, tracking down leads and clues to possible footage, particularly anxious to trace material from naval sources. Much of the surviving colour footage from the war years in Britain was in fact shot by an amateur, Rose Newman, with contacts which allowed her to shoot where others could not. Where possible, the Museum adds any background material or written records, sometimes enlists the film-maker to supply his own voice-over commentary. Both archives find that most people are rather gratified, as might be expected, that their films are to be given the dignity of permanent preservation. If possible, the archives retain the originals and provide the film-makers, or their heirs, with video copies.

Jerome Kuehl suggested that most of the amateurs active before the Second World War were either the seriously rich or people actually working in camera shops and their friends and relations. 'You get a rather odd social picture: the upper classes paddling at Monte Carlo and Deauville, or Jules and Gaston setting off on a bicycle tour of the Loire, taking their Pathé Baby from the shop.' The records made by the very rich were turned to splendid account by James Ivory in his *Autobiography of a Princess*, which used film from the collections of the Indian maharajahs. And in Britain there was also the alternative cinema of the 1930s, the films of social protest made by members of such groups as the Workers' Film and Photo League. Now that half the population spends its spare time making videos of the other half, the archives again have the possibility of more material than they could begin to cope with – or need to.

Some people think that things are already in danger of going too far. Victoria Wegg-Prosser, who has herself worked a good deal with this sort of material, spoke severely of the amateur movie fashion, arguing that most of the really valuable material from the past had probably been picked up in trawls by the BBC during the 1970s, when it was passed on to the Archive. 'Is the home movie material that is in the NFTVA catalogued? Do the present generation of people know exactly what is there? Has anyone ever looked at it?' With 'four channels pumping out domestic history every day of the week', was the record really in need of topping up? 'It's fashionable, it's available, but is it ever really going to be useful?' Television, she suggested, had itself begun with the social history, and slid to the trivialisation of jokey antics played for video cameras. The attraction of keeping grass-roots social history remains obvious, particularly perhaps for archivists looking for a change from the over-familiar. But the question has to be whether it will simply sit in the archives, little documented and unknown, until some distant researcher happens to stumble on it.

Both the major British archives act as agents for the preservation of official film records from the Public Record Office, adding yet another strand to the ramifications of storing non-fiction footage. The National Film Library, as it then was, came to be recognised as the archive for the purpose in the early 1950s, after a great deal of official dithering about its worthiness for the task; the Imperial War Museum was founded specifically to store official films. Because the PRO material includes footage shot by the Metropolitan Police (although not material coming from any other police force), the NFTVA is the unexpected, and by most people probably unsuspected, resting place for the police records of such catastrophes as the King's Cross station fire of 1987 and the rescue operations after the sinking of the 'Marchioness' in the Thames in 1989. Such material is embargoed under the thirty-year rule, as was film of the Suez campaign which was held by the IWM and released in 1986. Archives, however, do not expect the rush of journalists who head for the PRO when Cabinet papers are released. No one, as a rule, asks to see the previously embargoed film; possibly because no one knows it is there.

To avoid establishing yet another cache of film, with all its maintenance costs, these records are not held back, as the written ones are, but go straight into archive care, with the NFTVA and the PRO operating a joint selection policy. Once again, video has complicated the process. Any number of government departments, according to James Patterson, may find budgets for small videos, with no reason to record their existence centrally. 'The master material is probably left sitting at some little independent video unit. You can't track it down as you can with film.' All this material, in effect, washes around Whitehall – as, it would appear, it always has done. Is there yet another store for film and video too sensitive to be passed into the keeping of archives where staff have no security clearance? It is a possibility, although the general assumption is that government departments keep their own records. In any case, from the archivists' point of view, this is another case of material that has got away.

Archivists describe these developments, with a slightly uneasy optimism, as the 'democratisation' of film-making. Increasingly, it is slipping out of the grasp of the professionals, into a world where anyone with a camcorder could provide the unique moment in film history. No piece of film ever shot, after all, can have been analysed in such minute detail as the few fleeting frames of the Zapruder footage of the Kennedy assassination. The amateur colour film of Hitler at a Munich festival in 1939, shown by Channel 4 in the programme *Good Morning, Mr Hitler*, was a small revelation, with the softening effects of colour and a markedly unofficial shooting style reducing Nazi panoply to something more like a village pageant. It was, genuinely, history as not quite seen before, precisely because the viewpoint was not the correct one. But if archives are not simply in the process of piling up the unedited footage, amateur films, commercials, pop promos, video, greedily absorbing it because it is there, they have to develop methods of coping with where democratisation leads them, with everything that defies the formal and familiar categories. And this is bound to be expensive.

There often remains a slight suspicion that even in those archives where non-fiction and fiction, or non-theatrical and theatrical, film are given equal status, the unacknowledged preference will be for the latter; that if budgets ever became mercilessly tight, the art of the film would win out over mere history. The NFTVA operates on an even-handed basis, but even here there is one area in which non-fiction may seem to draw the short straw. The Archive has never seen it as part of its brief to try to round up films which have not gone through the normal distribution process in Britain. For years, however, there has been very little commercial cinema market for documentary; the major films have slipped into the country briefly for a festival screening, or they have turned up on television. A film by Chris Marker or Frederick Wiseman, for instance, will be taped as part of the process of recording television, and that version remains in the Archive. To go beyond that and make the effort to acquire a print would be an impossible exercise, using up a large share of James Patterson's meagre budget for purchases on a single title. The result, however, is that researchers studying documentary will have to make do with the video version – and think themselves lucky. For Godard and Buñuel, they would not be satisfied with anything less than the film itself; for Chris Marker, it's perhaps tape only.

'Of the scholars, nothing is to be expected, I am afraid,' Arthur Elton wrote in 1955. Scholars, in the sense of academic researchers, are still more likely to be interested in the fiction side of the NFTVA holdings. There remain the film-makers, the select but growing number of historians who have put together films for educational purposes, using archive footage, and the television programme-makers.

The problem for historians working with film is that the more serious they are, the more they can expect to run head on into the medium's most intractable features. Professor Donald Cameron Watt, who has himself worked extensively in this area, summed up one evident difficulty: 'To say things with pictures is rather a slow way.' Film may be usefully illustrative, but one picture is by no means better than a thousand words (or quicker) when it comes to dealing with diplomatic history or EU negotiations or the processes of economic change. Night after night, the television news bulletins wheel out their wallpaper footage, such as the shots of supermarket shelves which seem to accompany every item on the state of the retail market or the effects of inflation. The historian, however tenacious, is in something of the same boat, casting around for dramatic illustration, compressing a script savagely to fit the images, or allowing the connection between words and pictures to become slack and tenuous. Film has always been able to demonstrate the how much more easily than it has been able to comprehend the why: it is not a sophisticated medium when it comes to dealing with concepts or abstractions. And few film-makers have the time or the resources to let the visual material, rather than the script, determine shape and style.

History on television is another matter, because television by its whole character is the medium for the populariser: it can use film with an easier acceptance of its limitations, to illustrate and enliven rather than as a background to analysis. The craft of the great popularisers, men such as Huw Wheldon and Kenneth Clark, lay in an acute and subtle understanding of what television could and could not do, and the ways in which conventional wisdom could be sharpened and spruced up to give at least an illusion of fresh insights.

The high-water mark for the presentation of history on television, the most quoted of all British programme series, remains Thames Television's 1976 *The World at War*. It was one of the finest fruits of Jeremy Isaacs's regime at Thames; that he could never achieve anything on this scale at Channel 4 had largely to do with the economics of the medium. The special virtue of *The World at War*, apart from its scale, energy and self-confidence, was its concern about the facts of history. The programme-makers, and most notably the associate producer, Jerome Kuehl, wanted to persuade professional historians about the value of film as evidence – the old cause, this time taken up not by a pamphlet or an article but a practical demonstration. To achieve this, they had to treat scraps of footage with the same degree of respect that a historian would, or should, show to a document. They could not betray their sources by the familiar fudging: by the blatant (and usually self-defeating) ploy of flinging in a bit of fictional reconstruction when authentic footage of an action did not exist; by splicing together bits of two separate scenes to create an incident which might have happened but which no one had recorded; by illustrating something which took place in 1941 with footage shot in 1943. Their policy was that the film document had to be what it purported to be. If this involved major script difficulties, even pulling programmes apart and reconstituting them, so be it.

Not all film-makers agree that such things matter, or that juggling with footage rates as a sin rather than a peccadillo. The archives can be seen as the source material for other than historical truths – poetic truths, if the film-maker is daring enough to use the word – with film employed evocatively, to illustrate general themes rather than specific incidents. The difficulty, however, is that the film footage always does come down to a specific place and a specific time, and its manipulation on screen can seem like an affront precisely because of the ease with which it can be played with, and the mistrust this creates about its use.

Once material has been wrongly attributed, others will innocently repeat the lie: it becomes part of the record, until someone goes back again to the original source. Jerome Kuehl quoted one instance of a kind of unconscious deception.

It had always been assumed that Soviet footage shot at Auschwitz, and later used in compilations, dated more or less from the time the camp was liberated. But this happened during the middle of winter, and it was not until fairly recently that someone spotted a previously unnoticed clue. There are leaves on the trees in the film; it must date from some months later. Any honest programme maker, Kuehl suggested, would now have to take this into account by way of the commentary.

Getting things right involves scrupulous and detailed research, which does not come cheap. The example which always seems to be quoted is that of the researcher who can't trace any shots of a particular battleship but does find something on a virtually identical sister ship. The battleship is only going to be visible in long shot. Does it really matter? Yes, say the researchers and film-makers who care about such things, we're sorry, but it does. And nothing is more calculated to infuriate a producer, Kuehl said, than the news that the film needed to illustrate some particular point in the script doesn't exist: it means rewrites, frustration, the waste of time and money.

The World at War was made largely in collaboration with the Imperial War Museum Film Department, and in the course of production it performed its own kind of archival service, turning up rare material, including the footage that was not actually used, adding to the documentation on war and film history. Once it had laid down the rules, it might have been assumed that they would be acknowledged, if not always observed, that film-makers would find it more difficult to revert to the old dodges. This, of course, proved not to be the case. Kuehl suggested that although many film-makers try to observe the stricter standards, *The World at War* itself grew out of a particular production climate in British television:

> The executive producer in charge of the production had to be committed to scrupulous visual authenticity, and in turn that means he or she had to have persuaded the accountants that this was a worthwhile investment. Getting it right does cost a great deal more than getting it wrong. Because of the way archives are catalogued, if you want authentic material you have to know where to look for it, you have to be rather good at your job, and you also need to have the time and the leisure available to a print historian. This mixture of financial support, moral support and technical competence can only function in an atmosphere where such things matter.

The World at War was an expensive production in its day because of its scope and size. It cost some £2 million; and the equivalent at 1990s prices, Kuehl reckoned, would be close to £20 million. Always assuming, that is, that such a series could be repeated; the suspicion is that quite a bit of the footage they were able to draw on may have been lost in the years between. Producers in the 1990s with £20 million available to them are unlikely to think that a major historical series represents the most attractive option, even guaranteed world sales and long shelf-life.

Thames Television's *The World at War*

Kuehl produced a depressing forecast, as uninviting for the archivists as for the programme-makers:

> The cost of archive material, newsreel film, has actually increased rather less than the cost of most of the other elements going into TV production. It is *relatively* rather cheaper now to use archive footage than it was in, say, 1975. All the same, the cost has still increased to such an extent that it no longer represents a cheap option. You have the paradox that library footage is at the same time underpriced on its own terms and too expensive for its market. *The World at War* was attractive to the accountants at Thames because it could be made for substantially less than many other programmes. And that is no longer the case.
>
> You have something of a vicious circle. Archives will have to become more expensive, and as a result they are likely to be used less. And as a consequence of that, those using them will probably be less experienced. The programmes they make will not be so attractive, because they won't have the time to look for the new and interesting sources of material. They will continue to recycle the things they have seen before, simply because they know where to find them. Even I am doing this now – taping documentary material off the air with a view to finding the rest of the sequence to use it for some other programme: in other words, researching off someone else's programme. To have to use current production as a research tool because that is the only way you can afford to do the work – that's not terribly good news.

123

Murray Weston made a rather similar point, although in a much more optimistic context. He suggested that for academics and teachers, broadcasting can act as a 'conduit into the archives', that such programmes as *Secret History*, presenting the material pre-packaged, gave them at least a notion of what might be available in the kind of library where they feel ill at ease because of unfamiliarity with its technical language. Perhaps people do still need such guidance, easy routes into what are thought of as repositories rather than resources. It's certainly taking academics a long time to catch up with these forbidding places, now in existence for almost sixty years. And if television serves a useful purpose in processing material, which it probably does, it's evident that the standards applied to film remain altogether slacker than those applied to print.

The dilemma for the archives is that they cannot afford, as they never have been able to afford, to promote services which would buckle under increased pressure. As to the uses made of their material, they have maintained an attitude of strict impartiality, taking no position on the question of the legitimacy of all the forms of trickery available to film-makers. It is the essence of a national institution that it cannot afford to pick and choose between its users. At the same time, it might be open to an archive to signal preferences for the way in which material is employed, to indicate whether it takes the supermarket view of its resources, as goods to be picked up for any purpose by the casual shopper, or whether it regards them as film documents and primary sources to be accorded some respect.

The passive role has so far been the only one that the archives could probably have played. Television has scoured and scavenged and dug out the footage; archives have served it up. If television, however, is no longer going to have the time, the money or the motivation to do the spade work, then it remains for the NFTVA to explore for itself the lost continent of its factual film holdings. The Topical Budget book and video could be seen as a cautious but effective first step in this direction.

There might at some future date be a case for splitting the National Film and Television Archive into two distinct and separate sections: an archive along what one already has to think of as traditional lines, concerned with the art of the film and the integrity of the image, and a sister organisation dealing with all the factual and actuality material – television and video of course included. For reasons of economy, there is everything to be said for retaining one large preservation centre. But if archives come to be defined not only in terms of what they keep, but of who uses them and for what purpose, which might even be a logical extension of the emphasis on access, then there is a clear distinction between the two ends of the operation, and a blurred area in the middle which would present no insoluble problem. An archive serving journalists and historians – and, for that matter, scientists and sociologists and anyone else concerned with the factual record – might more easily adapt itself to demands for quick access, would not be bound by the old attitudes and inhibitions.

No one to whom I have suggested such a development, I should add, sees it as desirable, necessary or an improvement on the present state of things. It would, however, have the advantage of compelling the government to devote some attention to a question that has been consistently ducked, partly because the NFTVA has performed such a useful hold-all service. What kind of historical record should be kept, and what level of funding should be applied to it? This is, or ought to be, a national issue, involving the long-term future of a major national resource. Although at the same time, and given the way governments are likely to approach such questions, there could also be an argument for considering this an issue best not forced, for leaving the sleeping dogs peacefully in their kennels.

9

DEFINITIVE VERSIONS

In days of greater innocence – or, for that matter, ignorance – it used to be assumed in the world outside the archives that a film, more or less, was a film, a finite object. (The archivists always knew better; they had to contend with silent films, with their amoeba-like changes of form between different versions.) The film might have been snipped by the censors, or trimmed by its distributors to what they saw as an acceptable running-time; the blood quotient in horror films might be played up or quietened down according to the tastes of national markets. All the same, the ordinary filmgoer supposed that the form which a film took on its first release was the one it would retain to the end of its days.

Now, even the most ordinary filmgoer must wonder if there is such a thing as the definitive version of any film. *Dances with Wolves* seemed hardly to have left the West End before it was back again, with the threat or promise of 'over fifty minutes of previously unseen footage'. The de luxe or director's cut editions indulge auteurist conceits among Hollywood film-makers while getting more useful screen mileage out of the instant classics. Orson Welles, famously, found it more and more difficult to complete his films, leaving a trail of unfinished work in his wake. More recent directors get the film on to the screen first and then set about reworking it. Restoration in all its various forms, new ways of presenting old and not so old films, has become not only fashionable but virtually inescapable.

In archive terminology, a film which is merely held in safe keeping has not been preserved, and a film which has been preserved has not been restored. In theory, at least; in practice, the line between preservation and restoration is a little shaky. Preservation involves mainly technical decisions about what material to print from (the NFTVA's technical selection process) and is carried out to ensure the film a longer archive life. To get this far, as Clyde Jeavons put it, is to reach 'one level of expectation from an archive'. Restoration goes a stage beyond that level of expectation, the objective being to return a film as nearly as possible to its definitive form, if there ever was a definitive form which can be clearly established. The way a film was seen by its first audiences may not be quite the same thing, particularly if there were distributor cuts, and depending on whether or not these were approved by the director. Restoration means looking out not merely the best print in terms of quality but the most complete, restoring the shots and sections cut by censors or self-censoring film companies (*Spartacus*), bringing back footage jettisoned for reasons of length (*A Star is Born*), piecing

126

together several versions of a film from different archives. It can be a fascinating exercise in movie detection; it often has to be a collaborative one.

Restoration is seen as a somewhat pointless activity if it does not involve putting the film back into circulation. Archives engage in it for reasons of glory and prestige, self-justification and public approbation, as well as in the interests of the film itself. Film companies do it also for profit, which can be considerable. Anthony Slide in *Nitrate Won't Wait* quoted some figures: Columbia made $2 million out of David Lean's preferred version of *Lawrence of Arabia*; the release on videotape of *The Wizard of Oz* ('which required no restoration') brought in $10 million; *Gone With the Wind* cost $350,000 to restore and netted $7 million profit from the film and videotape versions (though the purists complained that the original colour, thought too garish for modern tastes, had been toned down). No commercial attraction can mean no restoration: Disney, for instance, showed no interest in a batch of early black and white cartoons found in the Dutch archive, leaving it to the Dutch to do the work.

A film should not be described as 'restored', properly speaking, if an archive or a film company has merely come up with a smart new print (and not all films, of course, call for any more drastic treatment). But even Clyde Jeavons admitted that 'you can call it restoration if you want to make a fuss over it.' Restoration is the word with a cachet attached, suggesting rare new footage, archaeological discoveries. Quibbles about precise wording are unlikely to stand in the way when there is a chance to score publicity points at a festival or elsewhere.

One has the impression that an archive these days which can afford to restore prints can hardly afford *not* to do so. This is the route to publicity, showing the organisation in its most positive light, another escape from the dull image of the mere preserver. But, as in so many areas, the archives took a long time to realise the potential of their holdings. For them, restoration only really began as a serious business in the 1980s. Before that time few would have had the resources, and those that did would have been nervous about the sort of publicity that now attracts them. And they didn't necessarily trust other archives enough to bring the secrets out into the open.

A pioneer in the recuperation, if not perhaps quite restoration, of films was the man the archivists saw as their most resolute enemy. Raymond Rohauer was an American who realised, rather earlier than most people, that there was some cash and glory to be earned out of silent films. His particular technique was carefully to research the background to a picture, snapping up rights which were obscure or had been allowed to lapse. He would then mount raids on the archives, brandishing his rights and demanding that they hand over their material on the film. The smaller and more timorous archives complained, dithered, in the end might feel forced to give way. Lindgren and the NFA were among those made of sterner stuff. When Rohauer turned up in 1971, asking the NFA to hand over its print of Douglas Fairbanks' *The Black Pirate* (and supported by formidable allies in Douglas Fairbanks Jr and George Hoellering, proprietor of the Academy cinemas), Lindgren was ready for him. The Archive had taken counsel's opinion some years earlier. The legal view was that the NFA was entitled 'to claim ownership and control of the physical material entrusted to us', that anyone who acquired rights in a film did not gain along with them the authority to claim the film itself from other people, unless they used it in such a way as to infringe copyright. (In a similar situation, in the early 1990s, the Belgian archive won the day in a case settled out of court.)

Most people, Lindgren drily noted, made their approaches in person. A lawyer's letter might be expected to follow if the initial effort failed. Rohauer's preferred tactic, on this and other occasions, was to fire a lawyer's letter across the archive's bows as the first salvo in a campaign. Later, he might appear in person and in a rather more conciliatory mood. Lindgren negotiated an agreement by which Harold Brown, working with experts from Technicolor, carried out the complex job of restoration, which involved working from negatives that were shrunken and incomplete. Rohauer paid £600 for his new print, and the NFA retained its preservation material and acquired its own viewing copy. The NFA might have chosen to go about the restoration in a different way, but it had repelled the shark and secured its position.

Rohauer's battery of expert lawyers could frighten the life out of the archives. He was able to keep *The Birth of a Nation* off many screens, including that of the National Film Theatre, for years during the 1970s. His claims might well not have stood up in court, but no one dared to put on a screening and take the risk of testing them in an expensive legal action. The archives had to admit their powerlessness. Yet, for all this, it was Raymond Rohauer who in

Our Hospitality: Raymond Rohauer brought back the Buster Keaton classic, but also changed its titles.

the 1960s brought back the full range of Buster Keaton's films, a tremendous feat of recovery and restoration, carried through with style, and re-establishing a reputation which, if it had never gone away, had been allowed to fade. There might be a slightly distasteful feeling that Rohauer was dragging ageing silent stars at his chariot wheels as he triumphantly paraded their films, but this not very appealing man had still done what the archives had failed to do – had not at that stage really considered as a possibility. It was not surprising that most archivists disliked him intensely, as the fox among the chickens, or that his ally should have been Henri Langlois. To be sure of identifying his own Keaton prints, Kevin Brownlow said, Rohauer was not above changing the wording of the titles, in *Our Hospitality* actually managing to lose the sense of the plot. This was very much a Langlois dodge.

Henri Langlois, who would always have been more of a restorer than a pre-server, never got very far in this direction. He did take some steps in recording a music track for Stroheim's *The Wedding March*, after first showing it to him at a projection speed so slow that the director complained his film was 'boring, horrible'. (For all his enthusiasm for silent films, Langlois was not much concerned with the refinements of projection speeds, and because he didn't like the intertitles reduced them to single frames.) Ironically, it was to help Langlois in his plans to work on Lumière material that Harold Brown devised his famous printing machine for coping with worn and aged film. This highly individual piece of machinery was largely put together from an old Meccano set, 'plus such pieces of timber and electrical plugs and sockets as I could find', held together with 'camera tape, rubber bands, paper clips and what the others insisted on referring to as knicker elastic.' It had no motor at first, because the NFA would have thought that an impermissible luxury; and it was for years an archive standby. The machine, however, was never used for its original purpose. 'This was the time of the great falling out with Langlois and we never copied any of his Lumière films. We copied our own instead.'

It took Kevin Brownlow's restoration of Abel Gance's *Napoléon* to wake everyone up, the archives included. This was more than a restoration: it was a romantic quest in its own right, a labour of singular devotion, as Brownlow worked patiently for years, piecing together scraps and shreds of film from all sorts of sources to reconstitute the lost masterpiece. The restored film's first screening in 1980, with an orchestra playing Carl Davis's score, was nothing short of a triumph, which spread from Britain to a range of international screenings and a somewhat shorter American adaptation. The charm of the exercise was that it had not been embarked on by an archive or a film company in the course of business, but by an individual in pursuit of a dream.

Yet, said Michelle Aubert, 'the work of restoration is never-ending, and particularly the work on *Napoléon*.' Archivists tend to the fatalistic view that the more thoroughly a film has been restored, drawing in all the available material, the more certain it is that a new and better print will put in an appearance. And an original nitrate print of *Napoléon* running to seventeen reels did turn up in due course – with a kind of absurd inevitability, in Corsica. It allowed

Abel Gance's *Napoléon*, restored by Kevin Brownlow.

replacement of the 9.5mm and 16mm sections. In the same way, Gaumont had been working for some years on its careful restoration of Jean Vigo's *L'Atalante* before it was realised that a better print than any to hand was just across the Channel, in the NFA. This was the original, unsubtitled print which the NFA had inherited from the Film Society, and it had remained unseen for the best part of forty years. The ability to call on such a print, for such a purpose, was a justification, David Meeker suggested, of the emphasis on preservation and the policies applied to it.

The NFA was less than hospitable to Kevin Brownlow during the early stages of his work on *Napoléon*. It was carried out 'in spite of Ernest Lindgren', thanks partly to some surreptitious assistance from Colin Ford, later head of the Museum of Photography, Film and Television at Bradford and then the NFA's deputy curator. At that time, the archives were not greatly disposed to sympathise with the work being done, still less with the troublesome demands made on them by the people doing it. They have had to learn better, and Brownlow was one of their teachers. After they had made the 13-part *Hollywood* for Thames Television, he and his partner, David Gill, went on to restore a whole range of films for the Thames Silents series. It's doubtful whether any of the television companies in the 1990s would feel able to embark on a kind of enlightened patronage which can bring so little in the way of market return, although the well-established Thames Silents in due course became the Channel 4 Silents.

After *Napoléon*, any archive with an eye to its public image had an idea of what the possibilities might be. An effective restoration programme, however, depended on several factors: sponsorship, film industry cooperation, closer relationships and working partnerships between the archives, all the elements which were gradually falling into place during the 1980s. The National Film Archive, for instance, concentrated on restoring British nitrate colour films, a project made possible by sponsorship first from Mobil Oil and then from the National Heritage Memorial Fund.

Michael Powell and Emeric Pressburger had reason to be grateful to the NFA for the restoration of their work – *The Life and Death of Colonel Blimp, The Red Shoes, Black Narcissus, Gone to Earth* and so on, brought happily back to their original glories. Rather casting aside its view that all films deserve to be treated as equal, the NFA undoubtedly played a major part in the rehabilitation of Powell's reputation, an enhancement of his standing as a film-maker which spread everywhere in the 1980s. Archives influence taste by what they choose or are able to make available; even more by what they put their weight behind. And this was a case in point.

The *Colonel Blimp* restoration was of particular significance for the NFA, and not only in its pursuit of Powell. It kicked off the British Technicolor restoration programme. Unusually, it received financial backing (£8,000) from the Rank Organisation. And the restoration was an interesting exercise in its own right. The film had been highly controversial (Winston Churchill, famously, had

Roger Livesey in *The Life and Death of Colonel Blimp*, the film which launched the NFA on its programme of colour restoration.

disapproved). It was also, for its day, unusually long – 163 minutes at its original (1943) screening – so that it had been more subject than most to later tampering. In his work on the history of the film, Ian Christie asked 'when, how often and by how much was *Blimp* cut?' He was unable to come up with conclusive answers, but pointed to an original running time for the American release print of 148 minutes and 'running times of 140 and 120 minutes...quoted by various sources'. (In the late 1940s, Rank even fought off an effort by the American distributors, United Artists, to bring out a 91-minute version.) 'By the early 1950s,' Christie concluded, 'it appears that either the US version had become the only one available in Britain, or that the film had been further shortened – possibly to fit into a double bill.' At this stage, and for many years afterwards, the full-length original would appear to have been nowhere in circulation.

The NFA restoration work was done in two stages. The first version, in 1978, was produced using prints which had been held at the National Film Theatre and passed to the Archive. Cut footage was restored (the print ran 'some 160 minutes'), but technically the NFA was not satisfied with what it had managed. The prints taken over from the NFT were by no means of pristine quality ('North of Watford prints,' as one of the experts disparagingly described them, rather than those beauties produced for a West End opening). For its second attack on *Blimp*, the Archive went back to its own original master material, which it had acquired from Rank in 1956 and which had remained unseen in its vaults. The second time around, the concentration was on colour values and grading. 'This was how we found out,' said Clyde Jeavons, 'that the soldiers' ceremonial uniforms were the glorious brand of scarlet and shimmering gold and that their trews were midnight blue rather than black.' It was 1985 before this second restoration, as close as possible to the original, was finally screened.

Modern laboratory techniques can occasionally achieve effects which actually improve on the original. For *Gone to Earth*, for instance, Michael Powell had felt that Mary Webb's heated rustic melodrama should emerge in a natural, inevitable kind of way against a background of russets and golds and browns – the colours of the autumn countryside. He put some of the indifferent critical reaction to the film down to the fact that this had never been quite achieved. It took the restored version, supervised as usual by the NFA's colour expert Paul de Burgh, to let him see something closer to what he had first envisaged.

But the film which perhaps set de Burgh and the other restorers the most tantalising problems was not a feature, but the Technicolor record of the 1948 London Olympic Games, which the NFA restored at the time of the 1992 Barcelona Olympics. This had been, for the time, a most unusual production, shot in colour in what amounted to newsreel conditions. Virtually every Technicolor camera in Britain had been called into service, some feature productions actually being grounded while their cameras were drafted to do duty at Wembley. Different film stocks had been used; weather conditions had been variable, often dark and drizzly. The whole thing set a restorers' conundrum of the first order. And, once again, new material turned out to be available: some twenty scenes which had been omitted from the original British release print, but which had been slotted into versions for other countries, as featuring their champions or their particular sports.

The NFA has restored other British colour films, from *Henry V* and *Saraband for Dead Lovers* to the lesser lights of *Blanche Fury* and *Jassy*. The film industry in Britain, however, has never been prepared to put much support behind such ventures. Rank has preferred to continue marketing its own prints of such films as *Henry V* and *The Red Shoes*, rather than putting the restored versions into general circulation. Such attitudes, which would be unlikely in the more co-operative climates of France and the United States, leave the Archive perhaps disheartened, but not surprised.

In France, Michelle Aubert has again made use of her archive's position as an offshoot of the Centre National de la Cinématographie: if producers and directors are worried about colour fading, as many are, it is for the French archive to work with them on collaborative undertakings. One consequence should be the chance to bring a film back into non-theatrical as well as general distribution, and an early example was the restoration of Jacques Demy's *Les Parapluies de Cherbourg*, carried out in cooperation with Demy's widow, Agnès Varda. 'I have decided on a complete and open relationship with the rights owners, when I can find them,' Michelle Aubert said of the general policy.

The UCLA archive, next door to Hollywood and the centre for high-profile restorations of American classics (*Becky Sharp*, first screened in the restored version in 1984, was one of the early ones), can follow a similarly cooperative policy. Really effective long-term programmes, particularly those involving colour films, probably have to depend on good relations with industries which can appreciate their value and also have an interest in looking after their own property. The whole business of restoration has been one of the factors helping to bring archives and industry together. And in this area, as in others, the American archives are helped by the survival power of the major Hollywood companies themselves, through all their changes of ownership and their boardroom conflicts.

Restoration, in any case, is no simple matter. The further back one goes, the less easy it may be to agree on the definitive version of a film; prints differing in significant respects turn up in different countries. The restorer may follow up clues, but often be left to depend on his or her own judgment. There are other problems, such as establishing a preferred or original version when a film has been extensively dubbed, with most of the cast mouthing languages not their own. There was also the habit, particularly favoured in Italy, of extracting double value from a subject, by way of a two-hour film and perhaps a four-hour television mini-series. The archives might well properly feel that they should keep both versions, but should they contemplate restoring both or attempt somehow to marry them? In general, however, the restorer's pleasure is in unearthing bits of footage which were abandoned or discarded, in establishing the longest version of a film. Pictures were often trimmed, after a sneak preview or a first screening, because scenes were found not to work with an audience, and by no means all directors would regard this as mere front-office interference. There is no particular virtue in length, and the strict discipline involved in getting through a story in ninety minutes probably did most films more good than harm, even if it left footage to be picked up and put back by enthusiastic restorers.

There were also Hollywood production tactics. Years ago, I remember watching the Hepburn-Tracy comedies *Pat and Mike* and *Adam's Rib* alone in a viewing theatre. I emerged with a sense of vague dissatisfaction: they had seemed less sharp, fast and generally dazzling than I had remembered them. With some temerity I mentioned this to the writer, Garson Kanin. His answer was one of those phrases that sticks in the mind: 'Yes, of course. Those films were cut for Radio City Music Hall.' Film-makers knew precisely when they might expect big laughs from audiences in big cinemas; and also that nothing was going to stop the laughter in its tracks more surely than the spectator's fear of missing the next joke. (The audiences, as well as the film-makers, were of course more disciplined in those days.) They therefore threw in the small dead spots, patches of padding, to allow the laughter to build and die at its own pace. One might be led to the shocking conclusion that these films, and other comedies from Hollywood's golden age, should not be added to in the name of restoration but judiciously trimmed to bring back the sense of speed and alertness, particularly if the new print is going to find its audience on video. No restorer would be likely to take kindly to such a suggestion: if added length is generally seen as a virtue, cutting is always seen as a sin.

Conscientious restorers can also produce versions of films which may be more satisfying to a researcher than to an ordinary audience. Peter Williamson's restoration for MOMA of D.W. Griffith's *Intolerance*, for instance, got round the problem of covering the several missing sections of the film by using enlargements from the still material originally stored with the Library of Congress to register copyright. (The marks left on the stills by staples were still in evidence.) This sort of restoration may more closely approximate in completeness to the original intentions, but can hardly avoid sacrificing some of the pace and rhythm. It is treating the film as a museum object for study rather than as something that might still be supposed to entertain. It's well worth doing, though it would be a pity if the film survived in no other form. With *Intolerance*, this is not likely. Clyde Jeavons said that there are at least three current restorations, none the same and each claiming authenticity. One reason was that Griffith recut the film as he took it round the country. In any case, this style of restoration is at the opposite extreme from the work done on Fritz Lang's *Metropolis* ('Murder disguised as restoration,' said Kevin Brownlow), where the Moroder score was an attempt to give a 1920s film some sort of fancy topicality for the 1980s.

Enno Patalas of the Munich Film Museum, an archive which has specialised in restoration work on silent films, argued that almost all such work in any case involves a series of hopes, guesses, compromises and approximations. You can never expect to revive the original object in its pristine condition, tinted and toned, with the intertitles retaining their often highly decorative style and with the appropriate musical accompaniment. Even if this were possible, the audience approaches the film with an entirely different set of expectations. Apart from

134

special occasions, such as the screenings of *Napoléon*, the audiences who go to cinemas to see silent films will largely be made up of connoisseurs. There can be no going back to what the original audience was seeing, to the sentimental simplicities or the stylistic sophistications.

Patalas quoted two examples of the kind of options to be considered. For the restoration of G.W. Pabst's *The Joyless Street*, he and his team were able to draw on prints from the National Film Archive, the Cinémathèque Française and Gosfilmofond (nothing from a German source). The Russian print was the most complete, having been exported before the German censors had done their work. It was also the most used and worn. In both the other prints scenes had been changed, and the order of sequences rearranged, because by the time these copies were made Garbo was looking a bigger star than Asta Nielsen and the narrative had been shifted around to emphasise her part. The scenario in this case enabled them to sort out the original shape and order; in other instances, with more intractable material, they could look to stills which might survive from missing scenes or to clues in the cueing of the musical score. The restorer's problem is to be sure that clues are pointing in the right direction, that changes from the scenario were not intentional, that discarded scenes were not thrown out deliberately.

The Cabinet of Dr Caligari must seem to most audiences one of the quintessentially black and white films of a black and white era. In fact, it not only employed the tinting and toning of an age which was never really black and white, but according to Patalas the actual colours – the usual blue for night and pink for

Greta Garbo in G. W. Pabst's *The Joyless Street*, restored by the Munich Film Museum.

boudoir scenes – were almost garishly robust. Two tinted prints turned up from the Montevideo archive. The first to reach Europe was badly shrunken; the second, from which a new negative could be made, was actually being used as a projection copy in Uruguay. To check on tones which had already begun to fade, with the blues edging their way towards green, the restorers were able to use an album kept by one of the early projectionists, who had snipped out some thirty frames as his souvenir. (This, incidentally, is a common example of how films lose some of their footage.) To complete the revelation of a pink and blue and otherwise coloured *Caligari*, Munich was collaborating with the archive at Bologna, which has developed special laboratory skills for handling such material. Tinting undoubtedly affects the impact of a silent film almost as much as the choice of music to accompany it, and some archives which had completed black and white restorations to their satisfaction may feel that they should finish the job properly. There is virtually no end to the tinkering that can be done with a silent film, as new material comes into play and more sophisticated areas of restoration are emphasised.

An enterprise involving the collaboration of establishments in Uruguay, Germany and Italy might seem a trifle exotic, but this is the way things not uncommonly turn out for the archives. One less far-flung but still intriguing joint venture may be carried out between the CNC Archive and the NFTVA. The silent film and equipment collection built up by a British enthusiast, Will Day, was offered for sale to the National Film Archive but rejected because Lindgren was unwilling to pay. It then went to auction, where it was bought

The Cabinet of Dr Caligari: restoration will bring back its original tinting and toning.

136

by Langlois. Since Lindgren had turned it down, Langlois no doubt felt a particular glee about acquiring it. Having done so, however, he never seems to have found time even to examine exactly what he had. Now that the collection is in the CNC Archive, Michelle Aubert has suggested that the two archives should explore it and do the restoration work collaboratively, perhaps applying for support from the LUMIERE fund.

Michelle Aubert argued strongly that no restoration project should be undertaken without some involvement from the film's country of origin. There is too much unexplored material which might not be readily available to an outsider, including odds and ends kept by the film-maker's family. The descendants of the Vicomte de Noailles, who backed Buñuel's *L'Age d'Or*, produced previously unknown material on a film which exists in so many different versions that it must be high on the list for those restorers most intrigued by mazes and conundrums.

In the view of Enno Patalas, the archives which actually show their films, and so have the most incentive to restore them, are always the ones with the best prints. Those that never show, he argued, have no reason to investigate, and consequently little idea of the completeness or otherwise of the copies they hold. The two main German archives, which will in due course be amalgamated as part of the reunification process, are examples of archives that concentrate on holding prints rather than screening them, as to some extent is Gosfilmofond. (Though Gosfilmofond's practice of keeping its prints largely under wraps had one rather fortuitous advantage, in that because they went unseen they were less subject to the whims and ferocities of Soviet censorship.) Munich itself is essentially an archive for restoration rather than preservation, where limited resources mean that negatives may have to be used for printing rather than as master material. But Patalas has the satisfaction that his films are shown.

The non-commercial outlets for restored films are limited but quite effective: festival retrospectives, special events of one kind or another and the archivists' own particular festival, the Giornate del Cinema Muto, held annually at Pordenone. Money may be as short in Italy as anywhere else for the day-to-day business of looking after films, but all sorts of special interest festivals have over the years sprouted and put down roots in small Italian towns, relying on a degree of local authority support almost unimaginable elsewhere. Pordenone, northeast of Venice, is small, prosperous, purposeful, and seemingly quite satisfied to house a festival inaugurated in the early 1980s by a group of young Italian enthusiasts who were determined that the occasion should become a model for documentation and research as well as for screenings. The books that have been published to accompany the festival's major themes have earned a reputation for meticulous detail and film scholarship.

Pordenone is a modest festival which has expanded to the limits set for it by the number of hotel rooms available in a town with no particular tourist attractions and the capacity of the rather elderly cinema used for its screenings. Many of the larger festivals have been so commandeered by the deal-makers that seeing films may be the last thing on many visitors' minds. Deals are no doubt made at

Pordenone, but they must be tiny ones. The long-lost cause of silent cinema commands the loyalty of a tireless, highly professional audience: it is very much the archivists' outing.

According to Paolo Cherchi Usai, who was one of the founders of the Pordenone Giornate, the festival has the leverage to persuade archives and others to look out unfamiliar material, to restore the films that it would like to screen, which are not necessarily the most obvious or fashionable ones. This purist among the younger generation of archivists was less enthusiastic about such events as CinéMémoire, the French showcase for restored films, which was launched in 1991 in a characteristically Jack Langian bellow of publicity. The CinéMémoire organisers, he suggested, tackled the archives as though they were raiding the shelves of supermarkets, greedy for treats. His concern, and that of some others, is that concentration on restoring films that can be presented as exciting events for a modern audience means neglect for the rest, that archives can be put under too much pressure to deliver their smartest wares.

Paolo Cherchi Usai named the Dutch ('they come up trumps'), the Danish, Swedish, Belgian and Finnish archives as among the slow but steady performers, unlikely to be distracted from pursuing their own programmes. As an Italian, he added, he had seen the United States as the model; after moving to Eastman House, he had a clearer view of the American problems. 'Eastman House has been able to do less work on nitrate in years than the Dutch have done in a month.' The argument that archives should not let themselves be seduced into following fashion need not be relevant if the restoration work emerges out of a solid basis of preservation, as the NFTVA can smugly boast. At some archives, the suspicion remains that preservation may be more talked about than practised; and if the restored films were indeed the only ones assured of effective preservation, then present policies could give short shrift to the rest. As in so many archive matters, perhaps because of the 'addiction to lying', it is unlikely that anyone really knows.

Cherchi Usai forecast that during the 1990s the pressure for more glittering and alluring restorations would increase, with heavy demand from the retrospectives which have become regular features of so many festivals. 'The fight for the premiere of a new film will become a fight for the first screening of the restoration with the most prestige attached to it.' Costs, already high because of the shortage of laboratories, would continue to mount. Laboratories kept going by an older generation of enthusiasts would go out of business or change their policies. Within a decade, he suggested, the reservoir of films able to carry the big occasion screenings would fast be drying up and a reaction would set in.

There are always archivists ready to come up with pessimistic forecasts. But in this case, some would say that the money for restoration is already becoming harder to attract, that the 1980s were the high point, apart from the work on more recent films carried out by the industry itself. Those archives trying to satisfy a demand for high-profile restorations can't really be blamed for taking advantage of a fashion which may well not last, particularly when any sponsor-ship money they can draw in is likely to be bound up with the gloss they can

Top: Charles Farrell and Janet Gaynor in Frank Borzage's *Lucky Star* (1929), restored by the Netherlands Film Museum and screened at Pordenone.

Bottom: *Nick Carter Le Roi des Detectives:* The NFTVA holds a section of Victorin Jasset's 1909 serial, also screened at Pordenone.

put on the enterprise. The film industry can still block efforts to put films back into circulation, by sitting on its rights even when it proposes to take no action; or it can move further into an area where video has opened up the market. But if an occasion such as the Pordenone festival brings lesser-known films (and those, of course, only silent ones) back into awareness, the further need would be for a worldwide network of specialised screenings which could pick them up and allow them some sort of circulation. It may be the growing problems in this area which partly account for the sense of frustration among some archivists, as they see only the cream skimmed from the top of the collections. Once again, the answer could be in video; but not many of the purists would like that.

10

KEEPING TRACK OF TELEVISION

Only a very few of the FIAF member archives keep television material. If they were offered the opportunity, and even the money to make it possible, not many more would probably jump at the chance to take it. Most, of course, are simply not big enough to think in such terms. But there is also the deep-rooted emotional loyalty to film, as the vulnerable and endangered medium, which in extreme cases leads some archivists to jib even at the evident conveniences of video. There must also be a strong suspicion that any archive which committed itself to television would in a fairly short time find that it had turned into a television archive, with film trailing behind as the fading, always weaker partner. The archivists' profession may be a young one, but that does not prevent them from being enthusiastic traditionalists: television is still seen by many as something new, unfriendly, threatening and best kept at a distance. As early as 1966, Grace Wyndham-Goldie of the BBC did in fact attend a FIAF meeting to discuss the question of television film material, for which 'preservation in terms of space and cost is creating an almost insurmountable problem.' The view was that each country's archive should work out its own approach; which would seem to have meant in practice that they preferred not to have to think too much about it.

The case for the film archives taking the plunge, or at least being prepared to get their toes a little damp, is plainly a strong one. The same people work in films and television, and there are directors who have arguably done their best work for TV. It would be invidious, for instance, to keep Jack Gold's cinema films and to ignore programmes such as *The Naked Civil Servant*; or to keep Kevin Billington's features and disregard his brilliant early documentaries for the BBC. There are even a few directors whose commercials might be more worth keeping than their features.

In production, too, there are an increasing number of technical crossovers: films can be shot on film and transferred to video for editing, or shot on video and transferred to film for distribution. It is already hard to draw clear demarcation lines, and will soon become even harder. A television programme could turn up in a cinema, though admittedly it would be unlikely; but any number of films are given their first screenings, which may well also be their last, on television or video. And if an archive had an established newsreel collection, and regarded the keeping of news film as a major duty, it had either to draw a line across its holdings at the point when the newsreel companies went out of business, or to follow the news into television. It is, of course, more than merely the news. The non-fiction

141

and documentary archive has also now effectively to be a TV archive. Only those organisations for which film has always and essentially meant feature production can really afford to live entirely by old loyalties.

Victoria Wegg-Prosser put forward a view which was very consciously that of devil's advocate. In so far as archives can be thought of as having a mission, having been set up with a particular purpose in mind, that purpose was the preservation of a film heritage. In time, the emphasis shifted: the 'heritage' was in effect redefined as nitrate. Once the nitrate problem has finally been eradicated, some time in the next twenty years, archives in countries with declining film production (most countries, in fact, other than the United States and some Asian countries) would find themselves with a much reduced role. Leaving aside problems created by the vinegar syndrome, their job would be to keep up with a fairly low level of current production. This, admittedly, is not a view most archivists would accept. But it sets a context in which television appears as a new challenge, if not a new goal.

The British Film Institute began tiptoeing towards television as early as the late 1950s. This was partly because the BFI has throughout its existence been an insatiably greedy organisation, determined that no scrap of what might pass for moving picture culture should remain outside its grasp, partly because even at that stage there was such an evident overlap with many areas of BFI concern. It was not too difficult, for instance, to forecast that what was still called 'film appreciation' was bound to expand into what came to be called 'media studies'. The Institute did not make an open show of its new television ambitions, but allowed them to slide into its work, including that of the National Film Archive. In 1959 the NFA appointed its first television officer, and in 1962 a television selection committee was added to the three committees long established for choosing films.

In archival terms, the early history of television more or less duplicated that of cinema, as a record of loss, neglect and casual destruction. Television is absolved of guilt for failure to keep its own beginnings: it wasn't possible. This was a live medium, and it was not until 1947 that fairly primitive telerecording techniques came into existence, at first consisting simply of setting up a camera and pointing it at a monitor screen. Some people have the illusion that they have 'seen' pre-war BBC television, when in fact all that survives is film taken to publicise and report on those first days at Alexandra Palace. When telerecording did come into use, it was not as a routine service but as a way of saving the relatively few programmes considered worth the effort. Television was the 'ephemeral' art, as it was constantly being described when it was not being called the 'wasteland'. And its early drama material was in any case so tied up with performers' rights and music rights that there was little point in preserving material which no one intended or could afford to use again.

What the BBC had in enormous quantities, even in those days, was film. When he wrote his 1955 article about archival material, Sir Arthur Elton described the BBC as 'probably the biggest single shooter of film in Britain', with an estimated 15 million feet of film already on its shelves and a further

142

100,000 feet arriving each week. 'The film to be preserved consists almost wholly of reels of *TV Newsreel*, sequences from documentary and other programmes sometimes made up almost wholly of film, and tele-recorded versions of live programmes. The last can scarcely be regarded as important archival material, except in so far as they contain material of prominent personalities of the day.' Elton, like the early commentators on film, could seemingly see no case as yet for keeping television other than for historical record purposes.

He was severe about what he saw as the shortcomings of the BBC system. The BBC library only received the newsreel material after it had been prepared for transmission, without a chance to look at the 'overs and cuts' which he felt were so necessary for building up a fully documented record.

> The BBC librarians appear to hold a status inferior to that of the directors and editors, and seem to be considered mainly as functionaries in a servicing department... Selection for archive and library purposes is as responsible and, in its way, as 'creative' as selection for editing. If a librarian is regarded merely as a lister of shots, pre-selected by others for purposes alien to his, all the best librarian in the world can do is to bring into existence a vast accumulation of listed shots, without plan or foresight and therefore, ultimately, with restricted usefulness.

Not many archivists, then or now, have been encouraged to play Elton's 'creative' role.

Film, at least, arrived at the library. Much of the rest vanished for good; as with cinema film, material was left lying around in odd corners, casually neglected, sometimes junked in a hurry to release storage space. Even after most television material was pre-recorded on tape, the habit of thinking of it as a live medium persisted. The idea of preservation and its careful habits had to be taught, according to Anne Hanford, head of the BBC library. And tape, although easier to keep, was also all too easy to junk, lose or wipe for immediate reuse. It was thought of as a production tool rather than as something to be kept, and the early years of tape remain one of the worst periods for the loss of programmes. All new television companies are bound to repeat the same experiences, said Anne Hanford: 'When a new organisation is preparing for a deadline to transmit, all its energies are going to be concentrated on that. But once you have transmitted your first programme, you've got an archive, whether you like it or not, and the sooner you come to terms with that the better.'

In *The Television Heritage*, a booklet published by the BFI, Steve Bryant, the NFTVA's Keeper of Television, listed an assortment of the programmes which had disappeared:

> 400 out of a total of 430 episodes of *Dixon of Dock Green* made between 1955 and 1976; the final four episodes of *The Quatermass Experiment*; several plays by Mercer and Potter; much of Armchair Theatre; most of *Sunday Night at the London Palladium*; *Tyranny: the Years of Adolf Hitler*, a 1959 ITV documentary

which featured an interview with Hitler's sister; James Burke and Patrick Moore's presentation of the first moon landing; Kenneth Tynan using a certain four-letter word for the first time on TV; nearly all of *At Last the 1948 Show* . . . just a tiny few examples from an enormous list which encompasses vast amounts of television entertainment . . . as well as the large majority of programmes transmitted live.

Television has a much poorer chance than the cinema of ever catching up with its missing past, though the NFTVA is in hot pursuit of it, with a search similar to the *Missing Believed Lost* campaign for films. Until the coming of the video-recorder, which arrived too late to be of much help in archival terms, there was no opportunity for the private collectors who salvaged so much of early cinema. Some 'lost' programmes have survived, by way of copies hung on to by the producers or writers or engineers. A *Steptoe and Son* episode which had been kept by the writer Ray Galton was recovered for the *TV Heaven* series. A few programmes may also still linger in far-flung parts of the world, perhaps playing out their time in small television stations; Steve Bryant mentioned an early *Dr Who* episode salvaged from Nigeria. But on the whole lost television is destined to stay lost, and in some areas no one will know exactly what has vanished until efforts are made to find it.

In television, it is not only the programmes that have disappeared, but many of the machines to play them on. During the 1960s and 70s, the standard format was 2-inch tape, first for black and white and then for colour; the industry then moved over to 1-inch tape, and more recently to half-inch. The notion seems to be that the working life of each format is turning out to be about half that of its predecessor. All these changes, which introduce greater flexibility for the professionals, make life increasingly difficult for the archivists. No one knows just how long the tapes may last: thirty years, with luck, seems to be an estimate for the old 2-inch ones. 'We could find that there is some terrible sort of time-bomb like the vinegar syndrome lurking in the composition of tape as well,' said Anne Hanford. 'We haven't seen any signs of it yet, or any warning symptoms.' As with film, the durability of tape probably depends largely on storage in controlled conditions throughout its existence, and on proper handling, 'which is just as important as storage and more likely to go wrong.' The newer tapes are less robust than the older ones, and even their containers are flimsier, increasing the risk of damage if they are thrown about.

Deterioration has been found in some tapes from the 1950s and 60s; and, for that matter, in some tapes from the 80s. ('The main tape problems,' said Henning Schou, 'are caused by binder migration and loss of lubricant. Cooking unplayable tapes in an oven can often make them playable again.') But the problem with 2-inch tape has less to do as yet with the collapse of the tapes themselves than with the shortage of machines for playing them. For some years the NFTVA has been acquiring old machines from wherever it can, cannibalising and reconstituting them. Sooner or later, however, the last machines will wear out, and the archives and libraries which have not already done so will have to face the need to transfer

Dennis Pryce and Yootha Joyce in *The Confidence Course* (1965). This is one of the lost Dennis Potter plays written for the BBC.

large stocks of material to a newer format. As with film, the longer they can delay confronting the problem, the better the chance that they may be able to solve it without finding themselves landed with yet another short-lived format and temporary solution.

Television companies everywhere keep great stocks of material, essentially for their own purposes: for repeats, for extracts which can be recycled in every kind of programme, and for sale, either for video or for foreign markets. Just as television gave the film companies a new awareness of the value of their libraries, so video opened up the market for the sale of old television shows – the Hancocks and *Fawlty Towers*, Inspector Morse and *Brideshead Revisited*, the timeless children's programmes and wild-life features. Television companies have paid more attention to their libraries since it became evident that they are such a source of income: someone will always want the early *Dr Who* programmes they recklessly threw away. Where the practice was to keep samples only from series, the whole run now has its sale value. But the television organisations, in Britain and elsewhere, at the same time made it quite clear that they were not in the archive business: they keep and destroy programmes to suit their own needs, and they saw no obligation to provide a service for journalists, researchers or anyone else who might want to look at material. The general public view of the film industry has always been that it is quite rich enough to take care of its own history; the same has obviously been true for television.

In the 1960s and 70s there seemed to be a certain amount of squabbling between the BFI and the BBC as to whether the BBC was running what the National Film Archive, from its own lofty perspective, regarded as a 'proper' archive. In fact, the BBC was for many years curiously coy about its own archival role. 'It took the view,' as James Bredin put it in his 1987 discussion paper 'A Television Archive for Britain', 'that its charter restricted its use of licence money to the making of programmes. . . At the same time, the BBC likes to regard itself as an international leader in archival practice [and] has long had an archival policy which is more responsible, enlightened and all-embracing than that of most if not all broadcasting organisations. . . It takes the BBC to live with such brazen contradictions.'

At the time James Bredin wrote his paper, the BBC held 500,000 cans of film and 100,000 videotapes and cassettes. As with most archives around the world, its policy has become steadily less selective. 'All kinds of factors are pushing the retention rate up,' said Anne Hanford; not merely the attraction of potential sales, but the reluctance of archivists to throw anything away. 'Most material of any consequence will now be kept automatically for at least five years.' BBC Enterprises, the commercial arm of the BBC, has its say in decisions about what to retain, and the decisions taken after five years about what to scrap will be considerably more cautious than in the past. There is even a fail-safe arrangement, whereby the NFTVA can have the chance of acquiring material which the BBC would be prepared to let go. The BBC also keeps the prints it has acquired of feature films, even if its rights to screen them have expired. The rights might always be renegotiated; a high-quality print, once surrendered, could be gone for good. On occasion, such films are passed to the NFTVA, with the clear understanding that the BBC can reclaim them. (This is another example of the lodging-house role played by the Archive; though a lodging-house which hopes that its residents are never going to leave.)

Sports footage, at the BBC and elsewhere, is treated as something of a special case: there is an immense amount of it, and it is likely to be used and reused more than most other material. So, except when sports coverage overlaps social and general historical concerns, which it not infrequently does, decisions about what to keep and what to scrap are more likely to be made by the BBC sports department itself. The theoretical possibilities are alarming. With a long-running event such as the Olympic Games or the Wimbledon Championships, there could be available for storage all the programmes actually broadcast, everything left over from the races and matches shown only in part or not at all, and everything shot by each of the several cameramen covering every event. Even the most thorough-going advocates of the philosophy that 'everything' should be kept (or, at least, that there may be a future use for everything that has been kept) must draw the line somewhere; and those who have retained their sanity would draw it a good way short of this point. Fortunately, most of this material is never going to get within range of an archive: it will be scrapped, reused and forgotten while the event is in progress. Though there is, I was told, a warehouse in Canada crammed with material from the 1976 Montreal Olympics – shot on old-fashioned film, therefore less readily scrapped, although probably much of it has little surviving purpose to serve.

Sports material has less resale value for the television companies than might be expected. The rights usually belong to the organisation staging the event, or may be tied up with sponsorship. But in itself it represents another huge resource. And it remains jealously guarded, if only because it stays in the hands of experts whose involvement with the material may be more personal and knowing than that of the regular archivists.

The commercial television companies in Britain have of course maintained their own libraries, with Granada – the only company to have retained its franchise throughout the entire history of commercial television – also having the most solid preservation record. All issues of *Coronation Street*, for instance, have been devotedly retained. When a company lost its franchise, there was nothing to prevent its library being sold or dispersed. It was Jeremy Isaacs's discovery of stores left behind by Associated Rediffusion after the surrender of its franchise, for instance, which led to this material being steered in the direction of the NFA. In effect, the NFA managed to creep into television archiving partly because of a growing realisation that all sorts of TV programmes had preservation value, partly because the commercial companies could not in the nature of things give the same guarantees of permanence as the BBC, and not least because the television companies, unlike the film companies, had public service responsibilities and could be called to account for them. If the NFA had asked for public money, in the form of an increased government grant, to diversify into television, it would probably not have got very far. The money was put up by the TV companies.

In 1969, the Independent Television Companies Association (ITCA) made a first modest grant of £10,000, enough for the NFA to acquire seventy-five pro-grammes from the various companies for preservation. The grant, once the principle had been established, increased slowly but steadily, so that the NFA could begin to build up what was at first a very small and extremely selective stock of programmes. By the time Channel 4 was founded and joined the scheme, the Independent Broadcasting Authority had already demanded that franchise holders should make arrangements both for the preservation of their programmes and for 'reasonable' security after the term of their licences expired. And in 1984, when the NFA was given permission to record material off-air, rather than having to buy it, the rate of acquisition leapt dramatically forward. When Steve Bryant wrote *A Television Heritage* in 1989, the NFA grant from the independent companies (including Channel 4) had risen to just under £300,000 a year, and it was able to record programmes 'representing about 25 per cent of the transmission hours for each channel'. (By 1993, the combined grant had increased to about £550,000.) Although, as Bryant added, it was only in a position to acquire material broadcast by the companies operating within its transmission range – at that time, Thames Television, London Weekend and Channel 4. There is still no arrangement for acquiring material broadcast by satellite. When the NFA felt that it should have football World Cup material, this had to be acquired by purchase.

The arrangement with the commercial companies suited everyone. In television terms the sums of money involved were very modest, permanent preservation of a decent percentage of television output was secured, and the companies had been relieved of any unwelcome pressure to open up their own

147

libraries or make any change in their working methods. The BBC, of course, stayed apart from all this, operating its own mighty archive while claiming that the terms of its Charter did not permit it to do any such thing, and widely regarded by television researchers as inaccessible, even secretive. In 1990 it yielded to the demand to make its material more available, and to that end entered into its own agreement with the NFA.

The BBC could, no doubt, have set up its own access department, but it would have been both a drastic policy change and an expensive one. Television companies do not want their libraries treated as a public resource: they are not geared up to that kind of interference with their own priorities. The NFA, which already had its video unit at Berkhamsted busily recording off-air, could take on the BBC programmes as well without any great additional investment. Accordingly, the Archive is paid a fee which was set for the first year at £40,000, to rise in line with the licence fee, to record all BBC programmes and to make them available to researchers and the like. This is essentially an access service, not a preservation one, and off-air recording does not in any case give preservation standards. It's an odd arrangement on the face of it, a kind of privatisation by the BBC, but one which greatly strengthens the Archive's hand in its bid to function as a television archive on a national scale. To signal its intentions still further, the Archive in 1993 added 'and Television' to its name, a decision regarded in television circles as long overdue.

It might have been expected that the new access service would be widely used, but this is apparently not yet the case. With so many organisations around the country recording television off-air for their own purposes, the programmes on offer are probably still too new to have escaped other people's attention. The service also crept in rather surreptitiously, unannounced and unpromoted, in the way things usually seem to be done in the archive world. The NFTVA's viewing facilities are quite modest; they would be under strain if more than half a dozen people wanted to look at videos at the same time. There is also the disadvantage that there are no funds available for cataloguing the BBC programmes, which have to be listed simply by transmission date. Any researcher, consequently, has to identify a programme by way of the *Radio Times*, a primitive method which collapses if the search is for a particular news item, or for a guest on a chat show. In that case, the NFTVA's cataloguers are able to refer to the BBC's own computerised records, the sophisticated database kept for its own purposes. This is another system which might not stand up to the strain of heavy demand.

Television studies are something of a growth area; although according to Elaine Burrows, who has charge of the access scheme at the viewing end, teachers are not picking up on the new service. They prefer to keep to the courses they know, where the material is already available: 'They are all still teaching Dennis Potter.' Historians and journalists seem to mistrust television as much as film as a primary source; or more probably have not considered it. As the stock of available material builds up, however, it is impossible to think that the service will not be in demand, unless academics find it easier to go on reading Hansard than actually to watch parliament in action. (The NFTVA takes

148

in material shot by the Parliamentary Recording Unit, including material not transmitted.) For the present, however, the demands on the NFTVA viewing service are for films rather than television.

A researcher trying to penetrate the BBC Library in search of older material would be unlikely to get very far. I asked Anne Hanford whether someone who felt it essential to see, say, twelve or twenty hours of programmes from the 1970s would be able to do so. The answer was a fairly decisive no; or only at a cost which would deter even the most well-funded. Scripts and transcripts could be consulted at the BBC's great paper archive at Caversham, which might be even more tantalising for the researcher.

To make such material available was not a BBC responsibility. It would be extremely expensive ('costs running into millions; a major commitment on a national scale'). Only persistent and influential pressure from those regretting the absence of such a facility, Anne Hanford suggested, might possibly have any effect; and such pressure is certainly not in evidence. A considerable range of old programmes is of course available, in one form or another: passionately and perpetually, the BBC recycles its own past. But although the notion that visual resources should become as accessible as print resources may be one of the archivists' dreams, it is not the most likely to attract public or political support. It's hard to resist the conclusion that this is a field where the suppliers may have to create the demand.

Murray Weston of the British Universities Film and Video Council mentioned that several of the universities which had paid fees of the order of £10,000 for the right to record off-air were doing little to implement a service, merely assembling the odd machine and a few tapes. Any educational establishment has this right, though no archives and libraries other than the NFTVA. ('My child's primary school can do it,' said Roger Smither, 'but the Imperial War Museum can't.' Or not yet.) To encourage universities to get more out of the resources they had paid for, the BUFVC launched its own back-up service, recording off-air and supplying the tapes to registered users. Tapes are kept for three months, giving even the most tardy the chance to catch up. This is not an archival function, but a practical link between worlds which the archivists try to bring together. If there is duplication in all this off-air recording and the listing and cataloguing that has to go with it, this merely means that visual resources are becoming a little closer to books in the way they are treated.

In his 1987 paper, produced on a Wolfson fellowship, James Bredin argued the case for a British national television archive to be operated by an organisation independent of the broadcasters. The National Film Archive had made so much of the running that it had to be the natural home for such an establishment. The assumption would be 'that the BBC and ITV will want to continue to operate their film and video libraries for their own entirely proper and legitimate purposes,' but that 'the contents of their libraries should also be made available to form the basis of a national archive.' Bredin asserted that the cost was 'no longer prohibitive', though without giving any indication of what it might be. 'The technology has now made it possible for us to preserve the originals and provide access to copies of everything we have kept of past programmes and everything we transmit from now onwards.'

Six years later, all these matters were still under discussion. James Bredin's suggestion that the cost would not be prohibitive somewhat clashed with Anne Hanford's view that the commitment would have to be a very major one. In its slow and crab-like advance across the years, to the point where almost all the elements for setting up a fully-fledged national television archive are in place, the NFTVA has managed to avoid the need to ask directly for much in the way of public money. It may well have assumed that this would not readily have been granted, though some public finance has been involved. Everyone is in favour of archives, provided that they don't have to foot the bills. And although it is mainly money from commercial television which has allowed the NFTVA to get so far, in striking contrast to the standoffish attitude of the film industry, the TV companies could hardly be called on to finance a national resource, particularly when their franchises give them no stake in the future.

As for the BBC, there is no suggestion that its material would be any more secure in a national archive than in its own hands, or that its selection policies differ in any significant way from those that might be followed by a national collection. The plus point for a national archive would be in the area of access, as the BBC/BFI agreement has recognised. Access to a national television archive is not only the key but, in a sense, the sticking point. At the NFTVA, where television acquisitions have been running at about 7,000 titles a year, or double the rate for films, a cataloguing backlog piles up. It may be easy enough to steer researchers towards the run of Dennis Potter's plays (or those that have survived), or to the well-documented drama series. Coping with the demands of the social historians who might be among the main users of a television archive is another matter.

The outstanding need, in fact, seems to be for a subject index covering the full range of film, television and video. Significantly, the BFI's computer system for film information, SIFT, was not designed with such a facility in mind. It would be an extremely expensive undertaking, like all major cataloguing operations, but it would open up the archive, particularly in television terms, as nothing else could. The problem with access, for all the archives and in all the areas of their work, is that, however much they talk about it, to make it really work requires resources beyond their means. It runs the risk of becoming something of a conjuring trick, a now you see it, now you don't illusion. Wistfully, they want to be used. Practically, they know they can barely afford to be.

Things are not necessarily better ordered elsewhere, although television is very much the area for specialised collections, busily recording and indexing material. The television archivists have their own international organisation, the International Federation of Television Archives, which was set up in 1977 after an abortive attempt to join forces with FIAF. In Anne Hanford's view, a single organisation might have been more powerful and influential. 'I preferred it in 1977 and I would prefer it now.' But there are 'still quite a lot of people in the film world, though not as many as in the past, who think that television is not quite respectable.' More significant, in practical terms, is FIAF's need to demonstrate to the film industry that its heart remains pure and non-profit making. To let in the television companies, with their dependence on sales – or, for that matter, any of the commercial film libraries – would change the character of FIAF beyond repair. A joint organisation remains an unlikely prospect.

In France, the major television archive is part of the Institut National de l'Audiovisuel (INA), an organisation comparable in its range of operations to the CNC. Collaboration between the film and television archives presented no problem, said Michelle Aubert, and she saw advantages in keeping the two areas separate, provided the archives worked together and exchanged information freely. Again, the INA operates commercially, in a way that the CNC Archive could not do. In the United States, the FIAF members with the largest television holdings are UCLA and the Library of Congress.

The Australian National Film and Sound Archive, based in Canberra, is one of the very few which covers the full range – including radio. It holds a total of two million titles, of which 55,000 are films; a clear pointer to the kind of imbalance which any combined archive would have to learn to live with, and which many would find so unwelcome. Henning Schou, who worked at the Australian archive before joining the NFTVA, spoke of the imperative need in such a situation for 'collection management' and suggested that the sound holdings presented the major problem – recordings snapped up from all kinds of sources, a vast accumulation of material, much of it unexplored. The television side of the collection is much more selective, being made up largely of runs of Australian serials. The archive only rarely records off-air. Interestingly, from a preservation point of view Schou saw closer links between sound and video, as the two electronic technologies, than between video and film. But the notion of drawing everything together, in one sprawling whole, must also involve differences not merely of technology but of selection standards and disciplines.

The National Archives of Canada, in Ottawa, also bring together film and television. The film and television side was created in 1971, initially as the official archive for the Canadian Broadcasting Service and the National Film Board of Canada. (The NFB, according to archivist D.J. Turner, 'did a better job than almost anyone else on earth' when it came to preserving its own material.) The other major Canadian archive, the Montreal-based Cinémathèque Québécoise, concentrates on film. Turner painted a familiar picture, of a period of rapid expansion followed by cutbacks in funding, of more and more material coming in with less possibility of handling and treating it adequately, of funds mainly available for those activities seen as directly serving the public. Not, said Turner, that the public is a large one: it amounts to 'a tiny minority of the population'.

The Ottawa archive is a government organisation, denied the possibility of attracting sponsorship to help finance its activities, but with the obligation, as a national resource, to let 'anyone look at anything'. This in theory, at least. In practice, it suffers from the usual shortcomings in back-up facilities, such as cataloguing. 'Part of the collection is catalogued to within an inch of its life; for the rest, no one knows just what is there.' Turner also pointed to another of the problems archivists regularly encounter: the computerised system which was hurried into place with too many errors built in to it, and with no proper paper trail leading back to the original sources. All in all, Turner took the view that 'television makes the problems of films look almost controllable' – not least because of uncertainty about the durability of tape.

Television does seem under control in New York's Museum of Radio and Television, because its concern is with access rather than preservation; Ronald Simon, the television curator, described it as 'among the leaders in using material'. It was founded in 1976 and supported by the William S. Paley Foundation, after the Museum of Modern Art had turned down Paley's suggestion that it might expand into television. The Museum's viewing facilities are generous and inviting, a far cry from the basement cubicles which are the best the NFTVA can muster, and programmes can be summoned up via a computer system, immediately in the case of material for which there is a regular demand. The Museum has no right to record off-air, or to show any of its holdings off its own premises: it's a facility for researchers, and educationally for parties of schoolchildren and the like. Its collection of some 50,000 programmes, including 250 items about President Kennedy, is a selective one, chosen by advisory panels, and it would keep episodes from series such as *Dallas* rather than the full run. It prides itself on its Dennis Potter holdings.

This tiny sampling of a few television archives barely indicates the scale of the problems of trying to contain the virtually uncontainable. Added to which, television is at once a much more localised medium than cinema, with many programmes broadcast only by local stations, and an international medium in a different sense, with satellite transmissions crossing national frontiers and people in many countries having easy access to another country's terrestrial services, as with the Danes and the Swedes. Television comes at the archivist from every direction at once, and has to be caught on the wing. How much of it is netted, collected and stored – or how much should be – remains partly a matter of luck, with practicalities defying the archivists' taste for order. To make it accessible requires funds of the kind that Jacques Chirac, as Mayor of Paris, put into the Paris Vidéothèque – more than the CNC Archive reckons to receive. A videotheque can of course also show films, but its greater use is in opening up television, unlocking the doors the television companies have kept bolted.

When the British Film Institute in 1988 organised the project 'One Day in the Life of Television', the NFA decided, to quote Steve Bryant, 'to collect and preserve every minute of television broadcast in Britain on that day, and the BBC, all the regional TV companies and all cable and satellite channels were involved. The result was the addition of a staggering 521 hours of television to the Archive's collection. . .'

Staggering indeed. However familiar one is in theory with the statistics, it is still a jolt to be brought up against the blunt fact that British television broadcasts in a single day more hours of material than the domestic feature film industry would reckon to produce in five years or more. The scale of the operation is so different that archive customs must also adapt. The modern film archivists' reluc-

152

tance to make qualitative judgments, their dislike of seeming to use a privileged position to impose standards, comes up against practicality and economics. In the short run, television storage is easier and cheaper, but the space available cannot be infinite, and storage is only the first of the considerations at stake. Much television will continue to disappear, and will not be greatly missed. One can say, however, that the opportunity to study Dennis Potter's work seems to be assured, at least until well into the next century.

THE DURABLE SUBSTANCE
AND THE INDEFINITE FUTURE

In 1948, when nitrate was still used everywhere for feature production, Ernest Lindgren wrote of the need for the archives to copy their decaying films on to safety stock, although 'in ten or fifty years time the scientists may have found an even more durable substance.' His fifty-year deadline is fast approaching, and as yet a more durable substance has not been put into service, although many would put their money on polyester, which has been in use for some years for release prints. So far, however, the archive copying is still from nitrate to acetate (even from acetate to acetate). The only new substance has been videotape – used not for preservation but as a tool for making films available. In one sense, there has even been a step backward: acetate is now known to be considerably less durable than Lindgren and the other archivists of the 1940s expected.

Within twenty years or less the archives will be freed from the burden of nitrate, which has so far dominated so much of their existence. Those with thorough preservation policies should have completed them; those which have not been able to preserve their films will find that time is taking the responsibility off their hands – nitrate can't last for ever. By that time, however, there seems to be every likelihood that the vinegar syndrome will be eating its way through the acetate holdings from the 1950s and 60s, quite apart from any further diseases of tape or film which may still reveal themselves. It seems almost unthinkable that the archives should have to embark on another huge exercise in the eternal business of copying. Or that, if it had still to be a matter of making new acetate copies of old acetate films, anyone would be prepared to put up enough money for it. Some time in the fairly near future, they will have to hope to be able to commit themselves to one of the potential methods for preserving film – except that it will probably no longer be as film.

At one stage, high-definition television shown on a big screen looked like providing at least part of the answer. With cinema-quality images on a cinema screen it could preserve film-going as well as films. Demonstrations have been so effective that people have even found themselves looking round for the projector which they knew could not be there. But such special occasion shows, still on small screens, require a great deal of elaborate equipment (as Brian Jenkinson, a technical expert attached to the NFTVA, put it, 'There's a lot of difference between a carbon arc and hitting a chemical with electrons'). There is also the gap

154

between television quality and 35mm quality. When I spoke to Tony Cook at Berkhamsted in 1992, he suggested that 'the amount of storage space and the speed of transfer needed to store or move around enough digits to recreate a 35mm quality film is actually still technologically impossible.' The computer, in other words, could not process the data fast enough to sustain persistence of vision. By 1993, with the introduction of Kodak's Cineon system, the technologically impossible had already become possible.

If the Japanese standards of television had been adopted generally, Brian Jenkinson suggested, high-definition television might now not be too far away as a system for use rather than demonstration. But all the experts I talked to agreed that its development would have to be by way of the domestic market, the main source of incentive and income for such technological advances now that there is no longer the old spending by the services and the space programmes. Even before the general slowing down brought about by the recession, there was not much evidence of significant demand for a better-quality television picture. Perhaps because so few people watch television with much concentration, much concern with the image as an image, most seem satisfied enough with what they have – even if that means an indifferently tuned set in a not very good reception area. In any case, in terms of this sort of domestic spending, the satellite dish probably remains first in the queue.

Eventually, high-definition television will stake its claim, but the development of a power source strong enough to make it viable in cinemas would be expensive and still seems a fair way off. Some doubt whether it would in any case be worth it, whether there is enough of a future for cinemas themselves to justify major investment. Don't many people already prefer getting together to drink and chat and watch a video, and won't the future lie with the mini-cinema in the home for anyone able to afford it, with the latest product of the family camcorder as part of the programme? But people have been talking for years as though the cinema was merely hanging on by its fingernails. One suspects that it will continue to do so for a good many years, with its old and familiar technology.

On the whole, the experts whose background is in television take a more optimistic and philosophical view of any impending developments than those whose thinking has been governed by film. The transition from a photographic system to an electronic one would represent an enormous change of direction for the archives (and for everyone else). It would be a burning of the boats, a commitment from which there could be no easy turning back. They have to be confident that whatever decision they may eventually make is the right one.

Everyone agrees that the technology has to be digital. The advantage of the digital signal is that it never changes, that every copy can be an exact repetition of every other copy, a true cloning. There is no colour fading, because there are no dyes to fade. The process of converting analog signals to digital, said Brian Jenkinson, 'is not error-free, but the error is so small that it's difficult to measure.'

The developments in digital technology are likely to come by way of film production, particularly since the electronically minded Japanese bought their way into Hollywood. If television programmes can be shot on film and

155

transferred to tape for transmission, films may be shot on video and transferred to film for projection. For the commercials, where the demand is always for effects that are compressed, sophisticated and dazzling, digital trickery has released the genie. Is the microphone visible in the shot? Don't bother: paint it out. Can I introduce myself as an actor into a film scene? Yes, you can, if you can afford a not very cost-effective operation. Within ten years, suggested Brian Jenkinson, there will be so much switching to and fro between video and film that very few people will be able to recognise any difference. And all these changes can slowly work their way back towards the archives. One possible delaying factor, suggest the television professionals, is the surviving snobbery of film, the notion that a film-maker may be an artist while a television director can never be more than a technician.

One major decision for the archives would be whether to use optical discs or magnetic tape. Discs have the advantage of speedy access. Clyde Jeavons forecast an admittedly distant though theoretically possible future, with all the holdings of an archive, or as much as it was worth its while to make available, accessible to anyone capable of pushing a button. It would be a 'super jukebox', a 'gigantic emporium', the ultimate dream of access. (Though there is also the question of the tiny minority at present served by any archive, and of whether the demand would ever increase enough to justify putting such a facility in place.) Brian Jenkinson saw tape as the likelier contender, at least in the short term, for any developments contemplated in the next decade. 'If you think of technology as endlessly advancing, magnetic has the greater potential, in terms of containing more visual information in a smaller space. With optical recording, the limit is set for you by the wavelength of light, and you can't go beyond that.'

As with film, there can be no certainty about how long any tape or disc will last. Archive terminology has changed, said Henning Schou. Expressions such as 'archival' are themselves no longer used. Definitions are in terms of the life expectancy of the dyes, of the film base, of the electronic software and hardware. To quote Brian Jenkinson again on the properties of tape: 'When you have a large quantity of chemicals spread out on the surface of a nice stable material, with every tape manufacturer having his own magic mix, you don't start talking about the stable material, you talk about this concoction you have put on it. Will it adhere to the backing material for a long, long time? When all the solvents have dried out, will the cohesion of the binder last out, or will it flake off?' Tape can have its own built-in early warning system, signalling its approaching decay.

All the electronic technologies have been changing much too fast for the archivists, with the new tape formats and exhausted machines. Brian Jenkinson came up with a splendidly absurdist forecast: that if the present rate of progression continued, with each tape format lasting roughly half the time of its predecessor, by about the year 2020 the format would actually change during the recording of a programme. The interests of the users of tape as a production tool are by no means those of the archivists, looking above all for stability and durability. They have to wait both for the improvement in the quality of the image, to bring the electronic picture into line with the standard of a good-quality 35mm print, and also for the technology to have reached a stage where it may seem to have settled down. The first condition is likely to be achieved more quickly than the second.

There remain large areas of uncertainty and considerable scepticism. Brian Jenkinson admitted that 'the television system has a drawback which no one mentions, which people prefer to pretend doesn't exist. And that is that it is unable to handle the contrast range of 35mm film, although it is getting better. In any case, film rarely uses its full contrast range, which is fantastic.' Other experts are more dubious about whether two technologies founded on such different principles can ever mesh to give an entirely satisfactory result. There are certainly archivists who would fight in the last ditch for persistence of vision and the 35mm image, and against anything which might debase it. And there are those, such as Robert Rosen of UCLA, who argue that the multi-media environment is a reality which they must come to terms with rather than 'moaning and moralising' about it. The general view has to be that the moaning and moralising will continue; but that the technology must win.

Such questions aside, the archivists have to contend with all their other uncertainties. 'It's not a good profession to be in,' said Anne Hanford ruefully, of librarians in general. 'There is no money anywhere, and it's getting worse,' was the dour summing up from Eva Orbanz, secretary-general of FIAF. 'The archives talk of a future in which they will show minority films,' said Paolo Cherchi Usai, 'but in many cases that future is already in the past.' Or there is the view that archives have played a central role in a network of activities: film societies, art-houses, specialised outlets for non-commercial films and so on. If these areas are contracting, with audiences dwindling and finance becoming more precarious, does this leave the archives themselves looking solitary and vulnerable? This is part of the background to their slightly frantic determination to demonstrate their services to the community. A strategy which works, as someone who might prefer not to be quoted by name put it to me, 'until some government minister looks into things and realises just how tiny that community actually is.'

On the credit side, they have achieved the kind of status and recognition which is not going to fade away, even if the money to support it does; and the very important goal of Statutory Deposit may generally be a little closer. Of the EU archives which answered a 1992 questionnaire, those in seven countries already had it, in one form or another: Denmark, France, Germany, Greece, Italy, Luxembourg and Spain. In Luxembourg, however, it had never been 'actually used' (most Luxembourg production is probably a matter of films flying flags of convenience); in Greece it was 'largely unused'; in Germany, Denmark and Spain it applied only to films which were in receipt of government subsidies – a large part of the Danish production, less so in Germany, where producers show the traditional lack of enthusiasm for extending the system. This leaves France and Italy as the two countries with a full statutory deposit system for national production in place, always assuming it is exercised. In the United States, the copyright registration system achieves much the same results, under another name.

The British Film Institute is optimistic that its latest set of proposals, in this

157

long-running story, may finally be attainable. This time, the attempt will be to secure deposit of the original negatives, not merely prints, of British films. When a film is 'the subject of commercial exploitation in the United Kingdom', the suggestion is that a mint-condition print should be delivered to the NFTVA within thirty days, and the original negative within, say, three years. The proposals extend to broadcast material. As to films imported from abroad, it is suggested that the importers should notify the Archive of their existence, with the intention that the NFTVA should have the right to receive a print if it requests one. There is also the proposal, already mentioned, that the Archive should act as guardian for films in cases where the copyright owner is untraceable. And there is a further suggestion that the Archive should have the right to request 'published electronic works' (which could include video games), which would be duly delivered to it if asked for. Given the rapid rate of obsolescence in this field, it might even be desirable to ensure an Archive claim to demand the machines for playing the games. Does the NFTVA really *want* video games? The position, it would seem, is not so much that it wants them as that it would like to put down a marker, securing its right to such material.

Once an archive has moved forward into television, it would appear that it can recognise no further frontiers, although video games might look an advance into technology for technology's sake. If the NFTVA is hopeful that it may be able to acquire the precious original negatives, the essence of the film which so few producers have ever been prepared to surrender, this has to reflect the changing attitudes of the film industry. There would probably be little objection from the film-makers themselves: most are now enthusiastic preservationists when it comes to their own work; and educated to the dangers. But directors have only a limited say in such matters. If the producers come to see this particular light, it will be largely because they can appreciate the benefits of having the negatives securely stored, at public expense, and with all the access they need for their own purposes.

Some twenty-odd years ago, Ernest Lindgren was firmly convinced that the tax-payer should not be expected to provide the film industry with what amounted to a free storage service. That was not at all the proper purpose of an archive. The NFTVA, and probably other archives overseas, has had to become altogether more accommodating in its attitudes. In one sense, free storage might seem the price to be paid for a really effective statutory deposit system, and consequently for ensuring that preservation funds are not wasted on copying indifferent originals. In another sense, it is only an extension of the already brisk to and fro traffic between the archive and the donors and rights owners. Archives may not exist to serve the film industry, but such a service, if the industry cares to call on it, is almost a by-product of the way they were set up.

Where the NFTVA has gone for growth in all areas, up to and possibly including electronic publishing, other archives may find themselves defining their functions more exactly, perhaps more narrowly. France probably understands better than most countries how to fit the arts into orderly bureaucratic structures. Michelle Aubert spoke of the need for 'clear cultural objectives and strategies to achieve them', for which the foundations were laid by the defined responsibilities of the three major French archives. Her own CNC Archive is the centre for preservation and the keeper of all the nitrate; the Cinémathèque Française concentrates largely on programming, as it always has done, with some educational work; the Cinémathèque de Toulouse sees its role not as confiningly regional but as broadly Mediterranean, an acceptance of the need for a centre specifically of the south.

Michelle Aubert described the CNC Archive as 'a home for orphans, for films which have lost their proprietors', which conveys a pleasing sense of a sort of Battersea Dogs' Home for the cinema. Jan-Christopher Horak also used the expression 'orphan cinema' of the Eastman House collection, but in a very different sense. His orphans were the films which he thought stood most risk of being neglected elsewhere: B pictures, small-scale independent films, the work of the East Coast independent film-makers of the 1960s and 70s, including documentaries. He had even persuaded some of the documentarists to put their original negatives on deposit rather than leave them to the mercies of the laboratories. This fits in with Mary Lea Bandy's emphasis on the need for archives to work with the living as well as the dead. Some countries can barely manage to support a single archive; it is in the United States, where there are so many, that greater specialisation seems possible, with each collection perhaps gathering in its own orphans.

In Europe, there have since the 1970s been vague murmurings about some form of grand and no doubt appropriately bureaucratic Euroarchive. Few would probably want it; and in any case the trend is less in the direction of centralisation than towards emphasis on the national heritage. The archives have become more internationally minded in their increasingly effective cooperation; less so in their preservation policies, in which the rule is every country for itself. Even those small archives with least hope of being able to preserve their films (for some, said Henning Schou, 'it's rather like trying to run an ice-cream factory in a greenhouse') seem unlikely to want to yield them up to larger centres. In the 1990s, if you want to keep films, you want to keep your own films.

It is not only the archivists who may feel like this. The New Zealand Film Archive holds valuable material on Maori life and customs, some of it dating from the 1920s. To the Maoris, such records of their past have an almost sacred quality. The Archive is the 'guardian of treasures of shining light', but it also ran the risk of seeming an alien place. To quote a Maori film-maker, Merata Mita: 'Too often, the collection becomes a process of selecting and arranging my ancestors' images to validate what is occurring, what the latest train of modern thought is in various academic fields of anthropology, history, sociology and so on. . . . The institution and not the living members of the family or the tribe makes the decision according to its own particular cultural values . . .' Jonathan Dennis, founder and former director of the Archive, realised the need to come to terms with such attitudes, to see the films 'not merely as ethnographic documents, but as living objects with their own spiritual energy.' The Archive had to take the films back to the people they came from, and in the 1980s found ways of doing this. For other archives and other cultures, similar situations must surely arise.

So far, the goal has been to collect and accumulate. Could the next century see the archives beginning to discard material? Museums and galleries have been under some pressure to unload the never to be displayed contents of their basements and backroom. Dead stocks look more wasteful than thrifty, and if this is a growing trend the film archives could not count on immunity. The area from which they might be able to shed material, with least risk of vandalism, might seem to be that of the factual film, often kept specifically for its subject matter. A black and white film from the 1950s looking at animal behaviour might well be worth keeping for its attitudes, or as an example of the techniques of the day, but time and newer techniques must have eroded the rest of its value. When it comes to newsreel collections, is it essential to keep every one of the many items in which ships were launched or regimental mascots paraded? When an archive has several different newsreel collections, duplication must be rampant, with each of the companies covering the same routine and familiar ceremonies – often with the cameramen standing shoulder to shoulder. In the case of wartime footage shot by pool cameramen, the shots would not only be virtually the same but exactly the same, the only variations being in editing and commentary.

Archivists are extremely reluctant to admit that anything in their care should, or even could, be discarded – hardly surprising, in view of the trouble they may have taken to get their hands on it. If pushed, they may concede that a case exists, but fall back on a second and more effective line of defence. To weed through material, even within quite narrowly defined areas, would be a laborious and expensive business, calling for an expert decision in every case. It is probably cheaper to leave it all where it is; it may even be cheaper to preserve more than might notionally be needed, rather than to select. Not all archives have the luxury of storage space to spare; but not all archives have large quantities of film which may have little left to say for itself. On the other hand, if old newsprint is to be preserved into the librarians' equivalent of eternity there is a case for treating old movie news in the same way.

When it comes to television, Gilbert Adair in a *Sunday Times* column produced an intriguing comment on the distinction between TV and film. 'Everything that happens in a film happens on the screen – there's nothing behind it, nothing beyond it. A television screen, by contrast, is rather like a window – we seem to be looking beyond the screen itself to the studio from which the programme is going out.' In the studio, some sort of event is being staged for the cameras, but 'it can nevertheless, as is not at all true of a film, be perfectly well experienced without them (that is, by being part of a studio audience).' From which premise, he went on to conclude that the value of old television shows, *Hancock's Half Hour* or *That Was The Week That Was* or a Dennis Potter play, is either nostalgic or sociological. 'We watch them exclusively as documents, documents in the dossier of our shared past. To those who did not share that past, they are almost totally without interest.' There is probably a good deal of truth in this, and in similar arguments that television essentially exists in the present tense, where cinema builds up history. So much television is a kind of gossip, than which nothing dates more decisively. This has nothing to do with the importance of preserving television; but it might indicate that nostalgic attitudes to old programmes differ in kind from attitudes to old films, and also that there comes a point when the nostalgia runs out and only the sociological interest remains.

This function of preserving the past, with a view to letting it out, if not now then at some future time, is not an easy one. A French critic, the late Serge Daney, took the view that the spread of the archive movement and of interest in film archives took place at the same time as the explosion in the quantity of images being produced all around us, and that the two things were by no means unconnected. The more uncertain we become about the value of all these images, or of *any* of them, the more assiduously we are likely to store them, in the 'secret hope' that they may have something to say to a future generation. If there is a philosophy at work here, it has to be that 'one never knows'.

In the early years of the archives, Ernest Lindgren and his allies believed that there could be an identifiable canon of significant work: the critical consensus might be fallible, but it was right more often than not, and in any case there was no prospect of keeping everything. For Henri Langlois and his faction, choice meant limitation and everything could turn out to have value. But Langlois' 'everything' did not stretch to round-the-clock television on many channels, promotional videos, surveillance cameras in shops and in the streets, patrol cameras on racecourses, the camcorder in the back garden. It was still a modest, confined, feature film sort of 'everything', not very alarming to anyone. Most modern archivists are Lindgrenians when it comes to the business of preservation; and most are followers of Langlois when it comes to deciding what to acquire and keep. To accept the responsibility of making choices, in an environment where everything is working against discrimination, seems to suggest that they think they know best. They shudder at the idea of elitism. But perhaps the time has come when we ought to ask them to take that responsibility, to choose a little more. Otherwise, those hypothetical future users of the archives, whose needs are so devotedly considered, will be left with an impression of a past that was all images, or windows on events, with every image endlessly repeating itself, and every window opening on the same studio and the same studio audience. Cinema is history: the rest is . . . the rest.

One returns, in the end, to Henri Langlois, and an unpublished article quoted in *Le Dragon et l'Alouette*. The first film archives, he argued, were the 'ultimate expression' of the movement which between 1916 and 1930 had created the art of the film; and if that art had not run into obstacles, there might have been no archives, because the energies behind their creation could have gone into film production.

Et je suis tout aussi persuadé que si les cinémathèques n'avaient pas été l'ultime refuge des amoureux du cinéma, elles n'auraient jamais pu bénéficier des concours qui ont permis leur développement et leurs victoires. Encore aujourd'hui, chaque fois qu'une cinémathèque perd conscience de ce lien avec le grand mouvement des années 1920, chaque fois qu'elle sombre dans une routine ou dans le conformisme, chaque fois qu'elle croit pouvoir cesser d'être la personnification de l'éthique la plus intransigéante et la plus sévère, en un mot, chaque fois qu'elle cesse d'être un oeuvre d'art en soi, elle voit s'affaiblir son enrichissement et ses moyens d'action.*

The archives did not only need their links with cinema's past and its history, but with the artistic morality of that past. The links are still tenuously there; and still needed.

---

* And I am just as convinced that if archives had not been the final refuge of lovers of cinema, they would never have had the benefit of the cooperation which allowed them their development and their victories. And today, every time an archive forgets this link with the great movement of the 1920's, every time it sinks into routine or conformity, every time it thinks it can stop being the personification of the strictest and most uncompromising ethical code, in short, every time it ceases to be a work of art in itself, it sees its treasures diminished and its effectiveness weakened.

Nitrate store at Gaydon

Books and Major Articles cited

Borde, Raymond. *Les Cinémathèques* (Editions L'Age d'Homme, 1984).

Bryant, Steve. *The Television Heritage* (London: BFI Publishing, 1989).

Elton, Sir Arthur. *The Film as Source Material for History* (London: ASLIB Proceedings, vol. 7 no.4, November 1955).

Eyles, Allen and Meeker, David. *Missing Believed Lost* (London: BFI Publishing, 1992).

FIAF (ed). *50 ans d'Archives du Film* (Brussels: FIAF, 1988).

Foxen Cooper, E. (article credited to 'A Correspondent'). 'Historical Film Records', *The Times*, 19 March 1929.

Lambert, R. S. *Ariel in All His Quality* (London: Victor Gollancz, 1940).

Lambert, R. S. and Price, Harry. *The Haunting of Cashen's Gap* (London: 1936).

Lindgren, Ernest. 'The Importance of Film Archives' (London: *Penguin Film Review,* No. 5, 1948).

Low, Rachael. *Documentary and Educational Films of the 1930s* (London: Allen & Unwin, 1979).

Matuszewski, Boleslaw. *Une nouvelle source de l'histoire* (Paris, 1898).

McKernan, Luke. *Topical Budget* (London: BFI Publishing, 1992).

Prolo, Maria Adriana and Langlois, Henri (ed: Sergio Toffetti). *Le Dragon et l'Alouette* (Turin: Museo Nazionale del Cinema, 1992).

Roud, Richard. *A Passion for Films* (London: Secker & Warburg, 1983).

Slide, Anthony. *Nitrate Won't Wait* (Jefferson, North Carolina: McFarland and Co., 1992).

APPENDIX
How Much has Been Saved?

To complement and underpin one of the main concerns of this book, film archives from all over the world affiliated to FIAF (the International Federation of Film Archives) were asked to estimate their success rate in acquiring and saving the film production of their own countries. Most of the established national or otherwise recognised archives replied (although Italy, with four FIAF member-archives, is a notable absentee), and what emerges from their responses, summarised in the table overleaf, is a rather sobering global portrait of (at best) semi-success – in some categories more than others – as well as the occasional disaster area (Japan, India . . .).

Film archives, by their historical nature, come in all shapes, scales and sizes, have varying policies and remits, and are mostly underfunded. Many, for example, have relatively large, eclectic, international collections of which the national production represents only a proportion of the whole; some others concentrate more, in varying degrees, on caring for the films of their own country. A few have systems of legal deposit which guarantee (for recent years, at least) a higher rate of deposit of national productions. But most do not.

For these, and several other reasons, the statistics gathered here are far from scientific, and necessarily hedged about with variables, uncertainties and approximations. It proved impossible, for example, to decipher accurately the extent of the loss of silent cinema in most countries (the picture is clearer in the sound era): most archives came late on the scene, when silent films were not only a thing of the past, but had already been physically destroyed or neglected on a large scale. One has to stick with the general assumption that, among the major film-producing areas in Europe and the USA, at least, some eighty per cent of silent cinema is irretrievably lost.

Nevertheless, the figures, compiled with the assistance of the National Film and Television Archive, tell a series of vivid local stories, particularly in the final column, and show the varying extent to which attention has been paid to the survival of our youngest art form in its first hundred years of existence.

CJ/NFTVA

165

	SOURCE	ALL FILMS		NATIONAL PRODUCTION	
Country	Archive	Total number of films held in the collection	How many of these form part of the **national** production? [Figures are mostly approx.]	How many of those are: a) features b) documentaries c) animation?	Proportion (%) of the country's total national production held in the archive: a) features b) documentaries c) animation
Angola	Cinemateca Nacional, Luanda	643	89	a) 4 b) 84 c) 1	–
Argentina	Cinemateca, Buenos Aires	11,850	910	a) 605 b) 250 c) 45	a) 30%
Australia	National Film and Sound Archive, Canberra	54,000	45,700	–	–
Austria	Fimarchiv, Vienna	40,419	75%	a) 45% b) 53% c) 2%	a) 60% b) 50% c) 40%
Bangladesh	Film Archive, Dhaka	916	70	a) 56 b) 14	a) 4.5% b) 6.5%
Belgium	Royal Film Archive, Brussels	35,000	15%	a) 85% b+c) 15%	a) 75%

166

Country	Archive				
Bulgaria	National Cinémathèque, Sofia	10,620	6,290	a) 490 b) 5,277 c) 523	a) 67% b) 75% c) 90%
Canada	Cinémathèque Québécoise, Montréal	30,000	11,000	a) 1,000 b) 9,000 c) 1,000	a) 70% (Québec) b) 50% (Québec) c) 80% (Canadian)
China	Film Archive, Beijing	39,373	19,199	a) 7,146 b) 11,286 c) 767	a) 31.95% b) 68.01% c) 0.04%
Colombia	Fundacion Patrimonio Filmico, Bogotá	100,000+	90% (incl. TV)	b) 50%	(total) 50%
Cuba	Cinemateca, Havana	8,782	5,374	a) 396 b) 4,709 c) 269	–
Denmark	Danske Filmmuseum, Copenhagen	20,000	2,800	a) 1,200 b+c) 1,600	a) 21% (silent) 95% (sound) b) 10% (silent) 50% (sound)
Ecuador	Cinemateca Nacional, Quito	458	97	a) 16 b) 75 c) 6	(total) 70%
Finland	Film Archive, Helsinki	82,134	31,463	–	a) 75% b) 70%

SOURCE		ALL FILMS	NATIONAL PRODUCTION		
Country	*Archive*	*Total number of films held in the collection*	*How many of these form part of the **national** production? [Figures are mostly approx.]*	*How many of those are: a) features b) documentaries c) animation?*	*Proportion (%) of the country's total national production held in the archive: a) features b) documentaries c) animation*
France	CNC, Bois d'Arcy	110,000	75%	a) 40% b) 58% c) 2%	a) 75% b) 60% c) 80%
France	Cinémathèque de Toulouse	17,130	9,500	–	–
Germany	Bundesarchiv–Filmarchiv, Berlin	141,500	132,000	a+c) 20% b) 80%	(total) 50%
Germany	Deutsches Institut für Filmkunde, Wiesbaden	10,000	60%	a) 70% b+c) 30%	(total) 10%
Greece	Cinémathèque, Athens	3,830	900	a) 600 b) 295 c) 5	a) 26% b) 12%
Hungary	Film Institute/Archive, Budapest	25,000	6,200	a) 1,079 b) 4,650 c) 450	a) 60% b) 46% c) 40%

Country	Archive				
Iceland	Film Archive, Reykjavik	500	70%	a) 140 b) 360 (inc.TV) c) 2	a) 40% b) 65%
India	National Film Archive, Pune	13,000	6,000	a) 4,000 b) 2,000	a) 6%
Iran	National Film Archive, Tehran	6,618	3,840	–	a) 80% b) 50% c) 50%
Ireland	Irish Film Institute, Dublin	3,000	2,650	a) 150 b) 2,400 c) 13	a) 25% b) 70% c) 35%
Israel	Film Archive, Jerusalem	18,000 (prints)	5,700 (prints) 3,200 (titles)	a) 645 b) 2,535 c) 20	a) 90% b) 55% c) 80%
Japan	National Film Center, Tokyo	13,522	11,980	a) 2,081 b) 7,511 c) 390	a) 7%
Korea	Film Archive, Seoul	3,134	3,134	a) 2,445 b) 689	a) 52%
Luxembourg	Cinémathèque Municipale	10,000	100	a) 20% b) 80%	a) 95% b) 50%
Macedonia	Cinémathèque	6,000	890	a) 40 b) 800 c) 50	a) 90% b) 80% c) 90%

Country	Archive	Total number of films held in the collection	How many of these form part of the **national** production? [Figures are mostly approx.]	How many of those are: a) features b) documentaries c) animation?	Proportion (%) of the country's total national production held in the archive: a) features b) documentaries c) animation
		ALL FILMS		NATIONAL PRODUCTION	
Mexico	Cineteca Nacional	8,500	6,000	a) 4,000 b) 1,950 c) 50	a) 65% b) 30% c) 5%
Mexico	Filmoteca UNAM	12,500	7,169	a) 4,214 b) 2,938 c) 17	a) 55% b) 28% c) 50%
Netherlands	Filmmuseum, Amsterdam	25,000	7,500	a) 1,250 b) 5,000 c) 1,250	a) 25% (silent) 80% (sound)
Netherlands	Government Information Service, The Hague	[45,000,000 ft of mainly documentary footage from Holland and former colonies]			
New Zealand	Film Archive, Wellington	18,351	65%	a) 1,160 b) 13,250 c) 110	a) 40%
Nicaragua	Cinemateca Nacional, Managua	533 (Somoza coll. 127) (Sandino coll. 99)	226	a) 9 b) 83 c) 7	a) 90% b) 95% c) 100%

Country	Institution	Total	Holdings	Percentages
Norway	Filminstitutt, Oslo	17,000	a) 590 b) 10,210 c) 50	a) 80% a) 40% c) 90%
Poland	Filmoteka, Warsaw	17,000	a) 900 b) 1,200 c) 210	a) 85% (after 1945) b+c) 10%
Portugal	Cinemateca, Lisbon	3,800	a) 200 b) 3,600	a) 25% b) 18%
Russia	Film Archive, Moscow	54,500	a) 8,000 b) 6,200 c) 2,052	a) 12% (silent pre-1917) 48% (silent post-1917) 82% (sound) b) 60% c) 70%
Spain	Filmoteca, Madrid	26,000	a) 6,700 b) 10,000 c) 300	a) 70% b) 70% c) 60%
Spain	Filmoteca Catalunya, Barcelona	50%	a) 55% b) 35% c) 10%	a) 65% b) 30% c) 5%
Sweden	Filminstitut, Stockholm	3,700	a) 1,500 b) 2,000 c) 200	a) 80% b) 5% c) 90%
Switzerland	Cinémathèque, Lausanne	35,790	3%	—

	SOURCE	ALL FILMS	NATIONAL PRODUCTION		
Country	Archive	Total number of films held in the collection	How many of these form part of the **national** production? [Figures are mostly approx.]	How many of those are: a) features b) documentaries c) animation?	Proportion (%) of the country's total national production held in the archive: a) features b) documentaries c) animation
Taiwan	Taipei	6,995	4,895 (films made in Taiwan & Hong Kong)	a) 3,100 b) 1,732 c) 63	a) 48% b) 49% c) 3%
Turkey	Film & TV Institute, Istanbul	6,000	5,000	a) 65% b) 33% c) 2%	(total) 95%
UK	National Film and Television Archive, London	220,000 (incl. TV)	75,000 (films)	a) 7,500 b) 66,500 c) 1,000	a) 17% (silent) 75% (sound) b) ? c) 25% (silent) 66% (sound)
UK	Imperial War Museum, London	30,000	27,000	a) 100 b) 26,800 c) 100	(good proportion of specialist production)
UK	Scottish Film Archive, Glasgow	8,000	3,000	a) 0 b) 3,000 c) 0	a) 0% b) 75% of perceived Scottish production

Country	Archive	Holdings	%	Breakdown (a/b/c)	Final column
USA	Film Department, Museum of Modern Art, New York	13,500	8,800	a) 3,200 b) 1,500 c) 400	—
USA	Library of Congress, Washington DC	505,000 (reels)	90%	—	a) 10% (silent) 50% (sound) b) 6% (silent) 7% (sound)
USA	UCLA Film and Television Archive, Los Angeles	39,000	33,000	a) 27,000 b) 3,000 (+ 27m.ft of newsreels) c) 3,000	—
USA	National Archives, Washington DC	55,000	97%	a) less than 1% b) virtually 100%	a) 0% b) 40%
USA	Academy Film Archive, Beverly Hills	12,000	95%	a) 75% b) 20% c) 5%	less than 5%
USA	Anthology, New York	6,000	90%	a) 4,000 b) 1,750 c) 100 (+ experimental: 2,000)	—
USA	Human Studies Film Archives, Washington DC	(8,000,000 ft)	95%	a) 12 b) 20%	(collections are of mainly unedited footage)

173

	SOURCE	ALL FILMS	NATIONAL PRODUCTION		
Country	Archive	Total number of films held in the collection	How many of these form part of the **national** production? [Figures are mostly approx.]	How many of those are: a) features b) documentaries c) animation?	Proportion (%) of the country's total national production held in the archive: a) features b) documentaries c) animation
Uruguay	Cinemateca, Montevideo	7,610	430	a) 58 b) 363 c) 9	a) 60% b) 10% c) 50%
Uruguay	Archivo Nacional de la Imagen, Montevideo	1,619	465	a) 109 b) 356	a) 30% b) 20%
Vatican	Filmoteca	3,600	200	b) 200	b) 100%
Venezuela	Biblioteca Nacional, Caracas	18,385	17,980	a) 920 b) 17,453 c) 12	b) 20%

INDEX

175

176